|| न हि ज्ञानेन सदृशं पवित्रमिह विद्द

MW00886240

Pūrṇa Vidyā

(Vedic Heritage Teaching Programme)

Bhāgavata Purāṇa

Part 4

"One's wisdom and appreciation of beauty manifests through various forms of one's culture. And the study of one's cultural heritage leads one to the appreciation of beauty and wisdom in life."
Swami Dayananda

Swamini Pramananda and Sri Dhira Chaitanya

Editor: Irene Schleicher

FIRST EDITION 2000
REPRINT 2001
REVISED EDITION 2004
REPRINT 2008
REPRINT 2009
REPRINT 2010
REPRINT 2011
REPRINT 2012

Published by
Swamini Pramananda and Sri Dhira Chaitanya

Books Available at:

In India

Purna Vidya Trust, Headquarters
"Mamatha", # 8A, Basement,
North Gopalapuram IInd Street,
Chennai – 600086 (India)
Phone: 044-2835 2593
E. Mail: **purnavidyachennai@gmail.com**

In U.S.A
E.Mail: **purnavidyausa@gmail.com**
Phone: 1-718-501-4785

In U.K
E.Mail: **purnavidya.uk@gmail.com**
Phone: +44-19522-73543

For more information on other Books/Cds/ Vcds of Purna Vidya visit the website: **http://www.purnavidya.com**

Printed in the USA –Charleston, South Carolina

सरस्वति नमस्तुभ्यं वरदे कामरूपिणी।
विद्यारम्भं करिष्यामि सिद्धिर्भवतु मे सदा॥

sarasvati namastubhyaṃ varade kāmarūpiṇī
vidyārambaṃ kariṣyāmi suddhirbhavatu me sadā

"Salutation to you O Goddess Sarasvati, who is a giver of boons, and who has a beautiful form! I begin my studies. Let there be success for me always."

Table of Contents

Message from Swami Dayananda....06
A Note to Children....07
Key to Transliteration....08

Bhāgavata Purāṇa

Introduction to the *Bhāgavata Purāṇa*....11
Story of *Dhruva*....13
Story of *Pṛthu*....17
Story of *Gajendra*....23
Story of *Hariścandra*....27
Story of *Gaṅgā*....32
Story of *Viśvāmitra*....37
Story of *Śakuntalā*....44
Story of *Satī*....48
Story of *Mārkaṇḍeya*....54
Matsyāvatāra....57
Kūrmāvatāra....62
Varāhāvatāra....68
Narasiṃhāvatāra....73
Vāmanāvatāra....79
Parśurāmāvatāra....86
Rāmāvatāra....92
Kṛṣṇāvatāra....106
Buddhāvatāra....127
Kalkyavatāra....132
Avatāra Review....136
The Incarnations of Lord *Viṣṇu*....138

Message from Swamiji

Dear Children,

Learning is play if you enjoy learning. Here is a book of learning made enjoyable. You learn Vedic Heritage through solving puzzles and playing games testing your memory and rational thinking. By studying this book you will not only learn Vedic Heritage, but also the art of learning. You have my best wishes and love,

Yours,

Sw. Dayananda.

A Note to Children

Dear Children,

Welcome to Part Four of the Vedic Heritage books. The study of these books will be the beginning of a journey of fun and learning for you! The book contains lessons and exercises based on selected stories of the *Bhāgavata Purāṇa.*

As you explore these pages, you will discover great heroes and heroines of the Indian tradition which include *Dhruva, Prahlāda, Hariścandra, Viśvāmitra, Bhagīratha, Kṛṣṇa* and *Kuntī.* The illustrations will help you visualise the characters and the games will help you understand their stories. You may colour the illustrations of the characters and their beautiful surroundings using your favourite colours. By playing the games, you will appreciate the attitudes and values of the characters and understand why they are role models for the Indian people.

As you listen to the stories in class, we suggest that you pay attention to the following details so that you can enjoy playing the games. Make a note of the names of the characters and places, and the relationships between the characters. Also try to visualise the scenes. Once you have recreated the stories in your mind, playing the games will be challenging and fun.

This year's curriculum also includes a play on *Daśāvatāra.* Significant episodes of each *avatāra* are brought to life through this drama. You can enact this drama at the end of the year and enjoy yourself and make others enjoy too.

We wish all of you fun and success in your new cultural expedition.

With love and best wishes,

Swamini Pramananda Saraswati

Sri Dhira Chaitanya

Key to Transliteration

Key to Transliteration and Pronunciation of Sanskrit Letters

Since Sanskrit is a highly phonetic language, accuracy in articulation of the letters is important. For those unfamiliar with the *Devanāgarī* script, the international transliteration is a guide to the proper pronunciation of Sanskrit letters.

अ	*a* (but)
आ	*ā* (mom)
इ	*i* (it)
ई	*ī* (beet)
उ	*u* (put)
ऊ	*ū* (pool)
ऋ	*ṛ* (rhythm)
ए	*e* (play)
ऐ	*ai* (high)
ओ	*o* (toe)
औ	*au* (loud)
क	*k* (skate) 1
ख	*kh* (blockhead)*1
ग	*g* (gate) 1
घ	*gh* (loghut)*1
ङ्	*ṅ* (sing) 1
च	*c* (chunk) 2
छ	*ch* (catch him)*2
ज	*j* (john) 2
झ	*jh* (hedgehog)*2
ञ	*ñ* (bunch) 2
ट	*ṭ* (start)*3
ठ	*ṭh* (anthill)*3
ड	*ḍ* (dart)*3
ढ	*ḍh* (godhead)*3
ण	*ṇ* (under)*3
त	*t* (path)*4
थ	*th* (thunder)*4
द	*d* (that)*4
ध	*dh* (breathe)*4
न	*n* (numb)*4
प	*p* (spin) 5
फ	*ph* (loophole)*5
ब	*b* (bin) 5
भ	*bh* (abhor)*5
म	*m* (much) 5
य	*y* (young)
र	*r* (drama)
ल	*l* (luck)
व	*v* (in between wile and vile)
श	*ś* (shove)
ष	*ṣ* (bushel)
स	*s* (so)
ह	*h* (hum)
ṃ	*anusavāra* (nasalisation of preceding vowel)
ḥ	*visarga* (aspiration of preceding vowel)

* No exact English equivalents for these letters

1-guttural; 2-palatal; 3-lingual; 4-dental; 5-labial

Bhāgavata Purāṇa

Bhāgavata Purāṇa

Introduction to the *Bhāgavata Purāṇa*

The *Rāmāyaṇa* and the *Mahābhārata* are epics, while the *purāṇas* are books of mythology. There are eighteen major *purāṇas*, all attributed to *Vyāsa*. There are also minor or subsidiary *purāṇas* known as *upapurāṇas* written by other authors.

The *purāṇas* are written in the form of poetry, although some of them carry occasional prose. They treat subjects such as *devatās*, *dharma*, cosmology and art. They also deal with mythological dynasties of kings before the historical period.

The *purāṇas* reflect the social, political, religious and artistic culture of India. The universal truths of devotion, justice and generosity portrayed by the role models in the ancient Indian context hold the same significance today. The narratives, therefore, form deep impressions in our minds.

To appreciate the puranic and the Vedic literature, it is necessary to understand the concept of the *avatāra*. *Rāma*, *Kṛṣṇa* and others are presented as *avatāras* in the *Rāmāyaṇa*, the *Bhāgavata Purāṇa* and the *Mahābhārata*. An *avatāra* means incarnation of the Lord. Even though the whole creation is the Lord, when the Lord takes a particular form for a given purpose, at a given time and place, we call that form an *avatāra*.

The puranic stories reveal that, before every incarnation, there is a collective appeal to the Lord in the form of prayers from the good people as well as the *devas*. They seek the Lord's help because the tyranny of the unrighteous people becomes unbearable and they cannot follow a life of *dharma*. These prayers become the *puṇya* because of which the Lord assumes a particular form for a particular purpose.

In the *Bhagavad Gītā*, the Lord gives three purposes for an *avatāra*: 1) to protect the people who are committed to *dharma*; 2) to destroy people's unrighteous acts; and 3) to re-establish *dharma* whenever it declines.

Story of *Dhruva*

STORY OF *DHRUVA*

Svāyambhuva Manu had two sons, *Priyavrata* and *Uttānapāda*. *Uttānapāda* married *Sunīti* and *Suruci*. *Suruci*, the younger of the two wives, was an attractive woman and *Uttānapāda* was infatuated with her. One day, the king keeping *Uttama*, his son, on his lap, was playing with him when *Dhruva*, his other son born of *Sunīti*, came running to the father to sit on his father's lap. *Suruci* pushed him aside and told him that he did not deserve to sit on the king's lap as he was not born of her. She sarcastically suggested to him to pray to the Lord and seek his grace to be reborn as her son. *Uttānapāda* observed the arrogant behaviour of *Suruci* but did not say a word to her.

Dhruva was hurt by the rude words of his step-mother. Crying aloud, he went to his mother. *Sunīti* embraced him affectionately and consoled him. She asked her son to accept the words of his step-mother and not bear any ill-feeling towards her. She told him that the king did not love her and thus *Dhruva* did not have any place near his father. She asked *Dhruva* to seek the grace of Lord *Nārāyaṇa* through austerities and meditation, as he alone could bring joy in *Dhruva's* life.

Dhruva resolved to seek the Lord's grace. He left the palace at once and proceeded to a quiet place. *Nārada*, who knew of *Dhruva's* plans, wanted to test him of his resolve, and met him on the way. He discouraged *Dhruva* from his pursuit by pointing out the difficulty in propitiating the Lord. He added that many great sages had even failed in their attempts to appease the Lord. He cautioned *Dhruva* of the sufferings involved in the life of austerity and advised him to be content with whatever the Lord had provided him in this life.

Dhruva was not convinced by *Nārada's* statements. He told the sage of his firmness in resolve to gain the highest end in life. He asked *Nārada* to guide him in his pursuit. *Nārada* was pleased to see *Dhruva's* fortitude and told him to follow the path revealed by his mother. He instructed him on the disciplines he had to observe and initiated him into the chant, "*oṃ namo bhagavate vāsudevāya*" - salutations unto Lord *Vāsudeva*. He also described the form of the Lord for the purpose of contemplation. *Dhruva* offered his salutations to the sage and left.

As per *Nārada's* instruction, *Dhruva* went to *Madhuvana*, on the banks of River *Yamunā* near *Mathurā* and spent the next six months in penance and meditation. The Lord decided to bless *Dhruva* without further delay. Seated on his vehicle, *Garuḍa*, he appeared before *Dhruva*. The form which *Dhruva* was meditating upon suddenly vanished and *Dhruva* opened his eyes. He was amazed to see the beautiful form of the Lord before his very eyes. He gazed at the Lord for a long time. The Lord knew that the child was unable to express his feelings or speak words of praise. He softly touched *Dhruva's* cheeks with his conch. At the touch of the conch, *Dhruva* poured verses extolling the Lord's glories. He offered his salutations unto the Lord and sought nothing else in his life except the constant remembrance of the Lord.

Story of *Dhruva* contd...

The Lord knew the purpose of *Dhruva's* penance. He promised *Dhruva* the rulership of the world after *Uttānapāda* and granting him an eternal place in the heavens, disappeared from his sight. After the Lord had left, *Dhruva* realised that he had not asked the Lord for *mokṣa* the ultimate end in life. He was sad about it, but decided to return to the palace.

After meeting *Dhruva*, *Nārada* went to *Uttānapāda's* place. *Uttānapāda* received him with all honours. Seeing the king unhappy, *Nārada* asked him the reasons. *Uttānapāda* then narrated the incident that had occurred with *Suruci* and *Dhruva* and repented for his inaction that had caused the child to go to the forest. He was anxious about *Dhruva's* condition. The sage assured the king that *Dhruva* would be protected by the Lord and that he would return glorious when the time was right.

At the end of six months, when *Uttānapāda* came to know about *Dhruva's* return, he went to the outskirts of the city with all the members of the family and subjects, and received him with all the royal honours. He embraced *Dhruva* with great joy and affection and *Dhruva* prostrated at the feet of his father and his two mothers. After *Uttānapāda*, *Dhruva* ruled the earth for thirty thousand years. He married *Bhramī* and *Ilā*. *Bhramī* had two sons *Kalpa* and *Vatsara* while *Ilā* had one son *Utkala*. At the end of his rule *Dhruva* renounced the royal life and took to a life of penance again. When it was time to leave this earth, the attendants of Lord *Nārāyaṇa* came and led him to the heavens and *Dhruva* received an eternal place in the heavens.

I. Fill in the blanks.

Complete the story by filling in the blanks with the appropriate words.

Sunīti	*Nārada*	*Dhruva*	sad
Uttama	pole	conch	pray
Suruci	*Prahlāda*	king	
	happy		

1. *Uttānapāda* had two wives, _______________ and *Suruci*, whose sons were *Dhruva* and _______________.

2. _______________ was the king's favourite queen.

3. _______________ was not permitted to sit on his father's lap.

4. _______________ dissuaded *Dhruva* from praying to the Lord.

5. The Lord touched *Dhruva's* cheek with his _______________.

6. *Dhruva* asked the Lord for the company of his devotees so that he could always _______________ to him.

7. Even though the Lord granted his boon, *Dhruva* was _______________ because he did not ask the Lord for *mokṣa*, freedom.

8. *Uttānapāda* made *Dhruva* the _______________.

9. *Dhruva* again prayed to the Lord and was given a special place as the _______________ star.

II. Questions to Stimulate Discussion

1. Have you ever seen the northern pole star? Look for it in the sky. What do you think makes it a special star?

2. What are the qualities that made *Dhruva* special?

STORY OF *PṚTHU*

Pṛthu was the son of King *Vena*. He was considered to be an incarnation of Lord *Viṣṇu*. *Pṛthu* was born, everyone on earth and heavens welcomed his arrival with joy, as they had been suffering without a king who could rule the earth.

At the proper age , the sages and gods performed his coronation ceremony and presented him with various gifts. *Kubera*, the deity of wealth, gave him a golden throne; *Indra* presented a beautiful crown studded with jewels: *Yama*, the Lord of *Dharma* honoured him with the royal baton to rule; Lord *Viṣṇu* gifted him his *Sudarśana* disc; *Agni* offered him a bow made with horns of an animal; Lord Sun brought for him radiant arrows; and *Tvaṣṭā*, a minstral of Lord Sun gave him an exquisite chariot. King *Pṛthu* received with humility the praises showered on him and sought the blessings of all the sages and gods.

As *Pṛthu* was named by the sages and gods as the protector of the world, he earnestly attempted to give protection to everyone. But his task was wrought with difficulties as his people were suffering due to the famine in his kingdom. They were starving and emaciated and began to approach the king for food. The king thought over the cause for the sufferings and realised that Mother Earth had withheld all the nourishment of the soil to herself, along with the foodgrains and plants. In his anger towards her, he took out his bow and aimed an arrow at her when Mother Earth, trebling with fear, took the form of a cow and ran for safety.

Pṛthu followed her wherever she went. Finding no asylum anywhere, she surrendered to the king and sought his protection. She pleaded that noble souls like him should not hurt her as the beings on earth would perish without her. *Pṛthu* replied that she deserved punishment for her indifference and disregard towards his people as she had not even provided the essential food for their sustenance. He, thus, persistently threatened her.

Mother Earth glorified him and told him the reason for her not providing the food. She said that *Brahma* had created the plant kingdom for the substance of the people, so tht they could live a life of good conduct and discipline. This meant also expressing their gratitude by observing the Vedic rituals, *yajñas* and religious vows, *vratas*. She added that people merely enjoyed Mother Earth s gift in the form of food, without leading a righteous life and without nurturing her. The plant kingdom was thus getting depleted. She had thus chosen to conceal the remaining food and nourishment in the soil and preserve them for sacrifices. She told *Pṛthu* to use the right means for drawing back the food from her. She asked him to find a calf, abefitting person who could milk her, and milkpot that could contain the milk. She pleaded to the king to level her surface so that rain waters would stay on her, rather than be wasted away into the ocean.

Story of *Pṛthu*

Story of *Pṛthu* contd...

Pṛthu patiently heard Mother Earth and agreed with her that the people had taken her for granted and forgotten her worth. She had been abused, mistreated by the people on earth. *Pṛthu* assured her that he would set things right. He made *Svāyambhuva Manu* as the calf and himself milked the cow and thus drew herbs and plants from her as milk, for the benefit of his subjects. He told everyone tht they, too, could get anything they wanted from her, so long as they approached her with a calf and a befitting milkman in reverence.

The sages milked her with *Bṛhaspati* as the calf and received the *Vedas* as the milk in the vessel of speech, senses and the mind. The *devas* milked her with *Indra* as the calf and received nectar as the milk in a golden vessel. The *gandharvas*, celestial musicians and *apsarās*, celestial nymphs, milked the goddess with *Viśvāvasu* as the calf and received the milk of sacred music and dance in a vessel made of lotus. Similarly, the *pitṛs*, ancestors and other animate and inanimate beings gained whetever they desired from Mother Earth. The domestic beasts obtained the milk of grass in the vessel of the forest with *Nandi* as the calf. The mountains received the milk of various minerals in the vessel of the basins of their ridges with the *Himālayas* as the calf.

King *Pṛthu* was pleased with Mother Earth. With his paternal love, accepted her as his daughter. She was henceforth called *Pṛthivī*, daughter of *Pṛthu*. *Pṛthu* ruled the earth with prosperity. He performed one hundred *Aśvamedha* sacrifices, a feat achieved only by *Indra*. *Indra* who tried to disturb the sacrifice out of fear af losing his status, finally surrendered and the sacrifice was completed. *Pṛthu* spent his later years in austerities and contemplation and finally left the world peacefully.

I. Mark the correct answer.

1. What kind of person was King *Pṛthu*?
   a. righteous
   b. mean
   c. selfish

2. King *Pṛthu* was sad due to famine and sufferingin his kingdom. The famine occured because
   a. Mother Earth refused to provide food for the living beings.
   b. the earth was flat.
   c. the bugs ate up the food.

3. King *Pṛthu* tried to punish Mother Earth because
   a. she was selfish
   b. he liked punishing people.
   c. Mother Earth was not performing her duty.

4. Mother Earth was not providing food because
   a. she wanted to be selfish.
   b. she felt abused, mistreated and harassed by people.
   c. she was hungry

5. Mother Earth was called *Pṛthivī* because
   a. she was the wife of King *Pṛthu.*
   b. she was the sister of King *Pṛthu.*
   c. she was the daughter of King *Pṛthu.*

II. Questions to Stimulate Discussion

1. This story teaches us to respect Mother Earth's gifts to us. What can you do to show your gratitude towards her?

2. How does nature nourish us through the sun, water, air and fire?

Story of *Gajendra*

STORY OF *GAJENDRA*

There existed a great mountain range known as *Trikūṭa* which extended to thousands of miles, surrounded by the milky ocean. In one of the valleys of *Trikūṭa* was a beautiful garden known as *Ṛtumān* which had flowering trees of all kinds. The garden was also the abode of many animals and birds and had an extensive lake which was full of lotuses.

In the forests around *Ṛtumān* lived a herd of elephants with their young ones. The leader of the herd, known as *Gajendra*, commanded total authority in the forest due to his strength and size. On a midsummer day, *Gajendra* was majestically roaming about in *Ṛtumān* when, oppressed by the heat, he desired to quench his thirst. Drawn by the fragrance of the fresh lotuses brought by the breeze blowing from the lake, *Gajendra* proceeded towards the direction of the breeze. He had a refreshing bath in the clear waters of the lake and quenched his thirst. Relieved of the fatigue, he began to play with his mates and young ones by spraying them with waters with his long trunk.

All of a sudden, a powerful crocodile caught hold of his foot with its mighty jaws. *Gajendra*, using all his strength tried to shake off the hold of the crocodile but failed. His companions too could not pull him out of the waters. Many years passed in the tussle between *Gajendra*, the lord of the forest of *Trikūṭa* and the crocodile, the lord of the waters of the *Ṛtumān* Lake.

Due to lack of nourishment and constant expenditure of energy, *Gajendra's* strength and spirits began to decline. The crocodile, being an aqua creature, doubled its strength by merely living in the waters. *Gajendra* saw his total helplessness and realising that the Lord alone could save him, sought refuge in the Lord.

The Lord came on his *Garuḍa* with the *Sudarśana* disc in his hand. *Gajendra* who was uttering the Lord's name in great distress, saw him and was relieved of his agony. The Lord extricated him from the jaws of the crocodile by ripping it open with his disc. The celestial beings rejoiced at the compassionate deed of the Lord and showered flowers from the heavens.

I. Fill in the blanks.

Complete the story by filling in the blanks with these words.

happy	*Ṛtumān*	quench
herd	crocodile	*Gajendra*
beautiful	Lord	*Aśokavana*

1. There was a _______________ hill named *Trikūṭa*.

2. On the hill was a garden called _______________ which had a big lake.

3. Once a powerful elephant, *Gajendra*, with his _____________ came to the lake to _______________ his thirst.

4. Suddenly a _______________ grasped _____________'*s* leg.

5. *Gajendra* prayed to the _______________ to be saved.

6. The crocodile was killed, and the Lord blessed *Gajendra* with a _______________ life.

II. Topics to Stimulate Discussion

1. The lesson taught in this story is that the Lord always answers the prayers of devotees. Share one incident when you prayed sincerely.

2. Give three reasons why a person should pray.

Story of *Hariścandra*

STORY OF *HARIŚCANDRA*

Triśaṅku, a king in the solar dynasty, had a son named *Hariścandra*. *Hariścandra*'s wife was *Candramatī*, the daughter of *Śibi*. As *Hariścandra* did not have any children, he prayed to *Varuṇa*, the deity of water, upon *Nārada*'s advice. Pleased with *Hariścandra*'s devotion, *Varuṇa* blessed him with a son who was named *Rohitāśva*. *Hariścandra* lived happily with his wife and son and he ruled the kingdom well. Sage *Vasiṣṭha* suggested *Hariścandra* to perform a *Rājasūya* sacrifice which he did successfully.

Vasiṣṭha and *Viśvāmitra* once met in heavens where *Vasiṣṭha* was shown preferential treatment over *Viśvāmitra*. *Viśvāmitra* questioned *Vasiṣṭha* regarding this discrimination. *Vasiṣṭha* replied that it was due to his association with the famous kings of the solar dynasty and his being the chief priest at the *Rājasūya* sacrifice of *Hariścandra*. He further added that there was no one equal to *Hariścandra* in nobility and truthfulness. All these factors had contributed to the distinct recognition that he received in the heavens.

Viśvāmitra became angry and challenged *Vasiṣṭha* that he would disprove *Vasiṣṭha*'s statement regarding *Hariścandra*'s character. He decided to stake his entire merits of his penances for this purpose. *Viśvāmitra* began to plan a scheme for depriving *Hariścandra* of his royalty and wealth. With his ascetic powers, he changed an *asura* into a hog and sent him to play havoc in the territory of *Hariścandra*. His attempts to drive away the hog having failed, *Hariścandra* set out to kill the hog himself. *Hariścandra* was driven far into a forest by a hide and seek game of the hog and before he realised, he had lost his way in the deep forest.

Viśvāmitra appeared before him in the guise of an old brahmin and promised to help him out. *Hariścandra*, pleased with the help of the old brahmin, offered to give him a gift of his choice. He took a bath in the nearby stream and taking waters in his hands, declared his intention to give anything that the old brahmin needed for his daily rituals or for any other purpose. Pleased, the brahmin requested help in the performance of his son's marriage. *Hariścandra* promised to help and both of them left for the kingdom.

Once they reached the palace, *Viśvāmitra* asked *Hariścandra* to give his entire kingdom with all its wealth. Deceived by the sage, the king was forced to part with the kingdom and his wealth in order to fulfill his promise. Customarily, no gift is considered complete without a *dakṣiṇā*, a symbolic sum. *Viśvāmitra* then asked for two and a half units of gold coins as *dakṣiṇā*. The king agreed, but he did not have any gold as he had just given away his entire wealth. *Hariścandra* was sunk in deep sorrow.

Story of *Hariścandra* contd...

As he was narrating his woes to his distressed wife, *Viśvāmitra* came and asked for the *dakṣiṇā*. Promising to give the *dakṣiṇā* at the earliest, *Hariścandra* left the kingdom with his wife and son, with clothes on their persons as their only possession. The sage pursued him with persistent demands for *dakṣiṇā*. *Hariścandra* vowed not to eat food until he had cleared his debt and promised to pay the *dakṣiṇā* within a month's time. The sage reluctantly agreed.

Hariścandra left for *Kāśī* with his wife and son, and tried to find some source of income. He was unsuccessful in his attempts. The sage arrived exactly at the end of one month and demanded his *dakṣiṇā*. Deeply distressed over her husband's fate, *Candramatī* offered herself to be sold to someone for clearing the debt to the sage. With tears in his eyes, *Hariścandra* went to a nearby village to sell her. *Viśvāmitra* had reached there ahead and appearing in the guise of a brahmin, offered to buy her and her child. Unaware of the brahmin's identity, *Hariścandra* sold his wife and son to him. The brahmin immediately caught hold of her hair and dragged her away with her child. Soon all the three of them disappeared from *Hariścandra's* sight.

Viśvāmitra again came before *Hariścandra* and asked for the *dakṣiṇā*. *Hariścandra* gave him whatever he had received from the sale. But this did not satisfy the sage as it was less than the promised amount. *Hariścandra* was given time till sunset to fulfill his promise. He walked along the streets auctioning himself for sale. *Hariścandra* was bought to guard the cremation ground and collect taxes on dead bodies. Thus saving some money he gave the remaining amount of *dakṣiṇā* to *Viśvāmitra* and was relieved from his harassment.

In the meanwhile *Hariścandra's* son *Rohita* died of a snake-bite while playing on the banks of Ganges. *Candramatī* lamented over the death of her son, but her brahmin-master would not permit her to see the dead body. He spoke harshly to her telling her that by *Rohita's* death he had lost his income and she had no reason to grieve. He asked her to go and do her work. He threatened to use his whip if she stayed on and lamented. Thus not seeing the dead body, as well as receiving blows for her repeated requests, she returned to her work. At night, when she was massaging the brahmin's feet, he told her to go and complete the funeral and return to work the next morning.

At the sight of her dead son lying stiff in the cold, she cried bitterly. Disturbed by her wailings, the neighbours surrounded her. They were convinced that she was mad and beating her, took her to the cremation ground to be killed by the guard.

Story of *Hariścandra* contd...

Hariścandra could not recognise her due to the change in her form. She too, did not recognise *Hariścandra.* When *Hariścandra* refused to kill a woman, his master handed him a sword and ordered him to kill her.

As *Hariścandra* raised his sword, *Candramatī* pleaded with him to wait until she had completed the funeral of her dead son. *Hariścandra* agreed. *Candramatī* ran to the town and brought *Rohita's* body. *Hariścandra* demanded the money for cremating the body. *Candramatī* replied that she had no money. *Hariścandra* then pointed out the *maṅgala-sūtra* which her husband alone could see. *Candramatī* realised that he was her husband. Both wept bitterly at their fate.

Hariścandra could not allow the funeral as he had to collect the tax from *Candramatī*. He did not want to deceive his master. As they could not afford it both decided to commit suicide before the night ended. A fire was prepared and *Rohita's* body was placed in it. As they were about to enter the same, the *devatās* appeared in the sky and prevented them.

They blessed *Hariścandra* and *Candramatī* for their commitment to truth and brought back their royal splendour. *Viśvāmitra* accepted defeat and returned the kingdom. The subjects welcomed their noble king with great joy. After his rule on earth, *Hariścandra* was given an eternal place in the heavens.

I. Storytelling

Form three teams. Follow the story to show how *Hariścandra* was tested for his truthfulness. The team which tells the story best wins the game. The story for each team begins as follows:

Team 1

One day *Hariścandra* lost his way in the forest and met an old brahmin...............

Team 2

To keep his promise, *Hariścandra* was forced to sell ....

Team 3

When *Candramatī's* son died of a snake bite ....

II. Questions to Stimulate Discussion

1. What do we learn from this story? Mark one answer.

   a. ____________ Truth wins sometimes.

   b. ____________ Honesty is the best policy.

   c. ____________ To succeed, one must lie.

2. Before you tell someone the truth, three factors need to be considered. They are:

   a. Is what you say true?

   b. Is your intention to hurt the person?

   c. Does the person who hears the truth benefit from it?

   Why are these factors important to consider?

   ____

   ____

3. Relate one incident to the class when you were honest, even though you felt like telling a lie. How did you feel about your action?

   ____

   ____

   ____

   ____

STORY OF *GANGĀ*

Sagara was a king of *Ayodhyā* in the *Ikṣvāku* dynasty. He had two wives, *Sumati* and *Keśinī*. *Sumati* had sixty thousand sons who were all valiant but arrogant of their power. *Keśinī's* son was *Asamañja*. *Sagara* arranged to perform an *Aśvamedha* sacrifice that was to give him the title, 'emperor of the world'. As a prelude to the sacrifice the consecrated horse was set free for capture by anyone who challenged the king's authority and sovereignty. The king would then fight the challenger and recover the horse. *Indra* threatened by the *Aśvamedha* sacrifice, stole the horse and concealed it in a cave.

Sumati's brave sons, honouring the wishes of their father, went in search of the horse. After searching all over the earth, they excavated the earth deep down in the north east direction. They found the horse standing in a cave near Sage *Kapila* who was in meditation. The sons of *Sagara* wrongly concluded that the Sage had stolen the horse and rushed towards him to kill him. Instead, they were instantly burnt to ashes due to the sin incurred in offending the great sage.

After a long lapse of time, *Sagara* became worried that his sons had not returned. He asked his grandson *Aṃśumān*, the son of *Asamañja*, to go in search of the sacrificial horse. Following the path dug out by his uncles, *Aṃśumān* discovered the horse in the cave near the sage. In his devotion, *Aṃśumān* saw Lord *Viṣṇu* in Sage *Kapila* and glorified him. Sage *Kapila* was pleased with *Aṃśumān* and blessed him. He asked *Aṃśumān* to take away the horse with him. The sage narrated the fate of his uncles and told him that the holy waters of *Gaṅgā* alone could redeem them from their sin. Offering his salutations to the sage, *Aṃśumān* returned with the horse. *Sagara* completed the *Aśvamedha* sacrifice. Soon after, he installed *Aṃśumān* on the throne and left the kingdom to live a forest life in prayer and contemplation.

Story of *Gaṅgā*

Story of *Gaṅgā* contd...

Aṃśumān could not bring the holy *Gaṅgā* in spite of his sincere efforts. In his later years, he handed over the kingdom to his son *Dilīpa*. *Dilīpa* was also unsuccessful in bringing *Gaṅgā* to earth. His son *Bhagīratha* was deeply committed to redeeming his forefathers from their sin and entrusting the rule of his kingdom to his ministers, went to the forest to perform severe penance.

Goddess *Gaṅgā* was pleased with his penance and agreed to descend on earth. The Goddess was concerned that in the absence of a restraint on her powerful descent, she might unwittingly break open the surface of the earth and reach the nether worlds instead. She also feared that the people there would wash off their sins in her and make her impure. *Bhagīratha* assured her that he would find a way by which her force could be held when she descended on earth. He added that even if she gathered the sins of others, she would always remain pure, by the sacred dip of the saints and sages on earth.

Bhagīratha then proceeded to propitiate Lord *Śiva* by performing penance for this purpose. Lord *Śiva* appeared before him and agreed to *Bhagīratha's* request to help him get the *Gaṅgā* descend without hurting the earth. As *Gaṅgā* descended Lord *Śiva* contained her force by holding her in his matted locks. *Bhagīratha* then led *Gaṅgā* to the spot where his ancestors lay in the form of ashes. Purified by the waters of *Gaṅgā*, *Sagara's* sons arose and ascended to the heavens.

Gaṅgā was brought to earth due to *Bhagīratha's* penance; so, she came to be known as *Bhāgīrathī*, one who was born of the efforts of *Bhagīratha*. *Gaṅgā* also acquired other names, such as *Ākāśa Gaṅgā*, one who flows in the heavens; *Tripathagā*, one whose path extends to the three worlds namely the heaven, the earth and the nether world; *Jāhnavī*, the daughter of Sage *Jahnu*; and *Mandākinī*, one whose flow is gentle (in the heavens).

I. Family Tree

Complete the family tree with the following names in the correct sequence.

Bhagīratha *Aṃśumān* *Keśinī* King *Sagara*

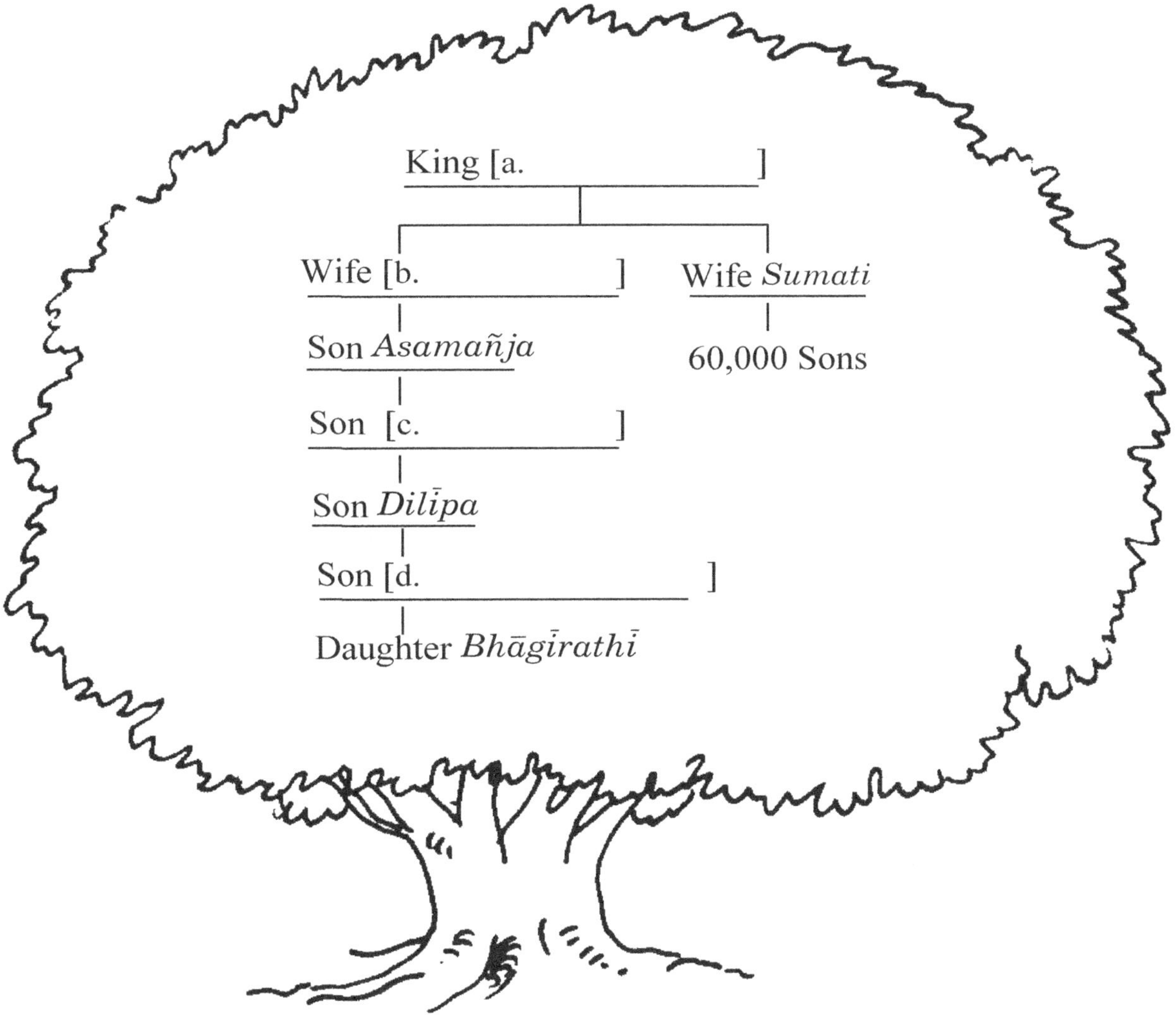

II. Mark the right answer.

Choose the four names of mother *Gaṅgā* and mark them.

__________ *Ākāśagaṅgā*

__________ *Maṇḍodarī*

__________ *Tripathagā*

__________ *Mandākinī*

__________ *Godāvarī*

__________ *Gāndhārī*

__________ *Bhāgīrathī*

__________ *Maheśvarī*

III. Name Game

Name a few of the sacred rivers in India. How many have you visited?

STORY OF *VIŚVĀMITRA*

In the lunar dynasty, there was a king named *Gādhi* whose son was *Viśvāmitra*. *Viśvāmitra's* earlier name was *Kauśika*. As a king, *Kauśika* possessed extraordinary qualities and ruled the kingdom well.

Once *Viśvāmitra* went on a tour of his country with a large army. As he was passing through a forest, he came across the hermitage of Sage *Vasiṣṭha*. The king entered the *āśrama* to pay his respects to the sage. The sage received him and offered him a grand reception, befitting a king. The sage requested the king to accept his hospitality and be his guest for the day. Concerned that the sage would not be able to feed his large army, the king declined his offer. The sage, allaying his fears persisted with his request and the king consented.

The sage called out for his divine cow, *Śabalā*. *Śabalā* arrived at once and awaited the sage's orders. *Śabalā*, the *Kāmadhenu*, was born during the churning of the ocean and was presented to Sage *Vasiṣṭha*. *Vasiṣṭha* introduced *Viśvāmitra* to her and asked her to prepare a delicious feast for the king and his entourage. *Śabalā* instantly fulfilled the wishes of the sage and an elaborate feast appeared before all of them. The king and his army thoroughly enjoyed the special feast.

Impressed by *Śabalā's* powers, the king asked *Vasiṣṭha* to present her to him as he felt that she would be more useful to a king than to a sage.

Story of *Viśvāmitra*

Story of *Viśvāmitra* contd...

He further added that anything precious in the country belonged to the king and thus staked a claim on *Śabalā*. *Vasiṣṭha* politely declined the king's request saying that *Śabalā* was inseparable from him. The king was displeased with the response of the sage. He offered huge wealth in the form of cows and elephants ornamented with precious jewels in lieu of *Śabalā*. *Vasiṣṭha* did not yield, when finally *Viśvāmitra* using his authority as a king, ordered *Vasiṣṭha* to hand her over to him. Seeing *Vasiṣṭha* defy his orders, *Viśvāmitra* got angry and asked his men to forcefully take her away.

Captured by the King's men, *Śabalā* broke down at the thought of being abandoned by her father-like sage. Wanting to know the reason for her abandonment, she released herself from the aggressors by force of her strength and sped towards *Vasiṣṭha*. *Vasiṣṭha* consoled her that he had not abandoned her and gave her permission to create an army to defeat the opponents. Defeated by the inexhaustible strength of the army brought forth by *Śabalā*, *Viśvāmitra* returned to the kingdom disgraced.

Viśvāmitra was determined to subdue *Vasiṣṭha*. He handed over his kingdom to one of his sons and went to the *Himālayas* to perform penance. Pleased with his austerities, Lord *Śiva* gave *Viśvāmitra* the divine *astras* as desired by him.

With his newly acquired strength, *Viśvāmitra* rushed to *Vasiṣṭha's āśrama* and unleashed his missiles at him. *Vasiṣṭha* understood what was happening and calmly placed his *brahmadaṇḍa*, the holy staff, in front of him. The holy staff swallowed all the missiles sent by *Viśvāmitra*. Stunned at *Vasiṣṭha's* power of saintliness, *Viśvāmitra* accepted defeat and returned with a determination to gain a strength which would match *Vasiṣṭha*, the *brahmarṣi*.

Carrying feelings of shame, anger and hatred, *Viśvāmitra* proceeded towards south and began practising his austerities in a quiet place. After a lapse of one thousand years, *Brahmā* appeared before him and conferred upon him the status of a *rājarṣi*, a royal sage. *Viśvāmitra* dissatisfied with the result, continued his penance with more vigour.

During that time, King *Triśaṅku* of *Ayodhyā*, once entertained a desire to ascend the heavens in his human form. His *guru*, *Vasiṣṭha* pointed out the impossibility of fulfilling his desire. Committed to his desire, *Triśaṅku* decided to find another *guru* for help. Soon he came across Sage *Viśvāmitra*. Prompted by his personal enmity with *Vasiṣṭha*, *Viśvāmitra* decided to prove himself better than *Vasiṣṭha* by fulfilling *Triśaṅku's* request. He accepted the challenge and took *Triśaṅku* to his *āśrama*.

Story of *Viśvāmitra* contd...

Viśvāmitra asked his disciples to arrange for a sacrifice that would send *Triśaṅku* to the heavens. Offering the oblations, he invoked the deities but no one appeared to receive the offerings. *Viśvāmitra* got angry and using all his powers acquired through austerities, commanded *Triśaṅku* to rise up to the heavens. To the amazement of all, *Triśaṅku* rose up in the sky and proceeded towards the heavens. *Indra* and the other *devas* could not admit him in the heavens with the human form and they pushed him down. Falling with head down, *Triśaṅku* cried out for help. *Viśvāmitra* was angry that *Triśaṅku* was denied entry in the heavens. With his powers, he arrested *Triśaṅku's* fall midway in space and created a separate heaven for *Triśaṅku*, known as *Triśaṅku -svarga*.

Having spent all his powers, *Viśvāmitra* went westward and reached a place called *Puṣkara*, where he again began performing penance. While he was absorbed in his penance, a young boy came to him with tears in his eyes. Disturbed by the sobbing of the boy, *Viśvāmitra* opened his eyes. The young lad introduced himself as *Śunaśśepha*, son of *Ajīgarta*. He said that he had been bought by Prince *Rohita*, son of *Hariścandra*, to be offered in a sacrifice being performed by *Hariścandra*.

Śunaśśepha was the middle son of *Ajīgarta*, who was a brahmin. *Rohita* had been looking for a boy who could be offered in his father's sacrifice in lieu of him. He had approached *Śunaśśepha's* father for one of his three sons in exchange for one thousand cows. The father had replied that the eldest son was dear to him, while the mother expressed that the youngest was dear to him. *Śunaśśepha* had felt abandoned and had offered to go with *Rohita*. On their way, they had reached *Puṣkara* and here *Śunaśśepha* sought *Viśvāmitra's* help.

Viśvāmitra adopted *Śunaśśepha* as his own son. He taught *Śunaśśepha* two *mantras* and asked him to chant them mentally when he was tied to the sacrificial post. By doing so, the sacrifice would stand successfully performed, without the loss of his life. *Śunaśśepha* was thus saved with *Viśvāmitra's* grace and the *yajña* was completed.

Viśvāmitra then continued his penance for one thousand years. *Brahmā* blessed him with the title of *ṛṣi*, a sage. Still dissatisfied, he continued his penance with more intense forms of disciplines. *Indra* became worried at the intensity of the penance and sent *Menakā*, a celestial nymph to disturb *Viśvāmitra*. *Viśvāmitra*, captured by her beauty, spent ten years with her and also had a child named *Śakuntalā* during this period.

Story of *Viśvāmitra* contd...

Viśvāmitra later realised his mistake and continued his penance, but this time, on the banks of River *Kauśikī* in the north. Lord *Brahmā* again appeared before him and blessed him with the status of a *maharṣi*, a great sage. *Viśvāmitra* wanted to know if being a *maharṣi* would give mastery over his mind and senses. Lord *Brahmā* replied that it would not and asked *Viśvāmitra* to continue with his austerities.

As his penance began, *Indra* sent another beautiful heavenly damsel *Rambhā*, to distract the sage. *Viśvāmitra*, committed to his resolve, sensed that it was the work of *Indra*. He was not captured by her beauty; instead he succumbed to his anger. He cursed *Rambhā* to become a stone and remain on earth for one thousand years. Immediately after, he repented for his action and realised that he did not yet have mastery over his emotions. He decided to pursue his life of austerity until his goal was achieved.

Viśvāmitra went east and performed penance for another one thousand years. Pleased with his firmness of resolve, Lord *Brahmā* granted his request and conferred upon him the status of a *brahmarṣi*. As desired by *Viśvāmitra*, he called his son *Vasiṣṭha* and asked him to acknowledge *Viśvāmitra* as a *brahmarṣi*. Seeing the spiritual growth and inner transformation in *Viśvāmitra*, *Vasiṣṭha* happily did so. *Viśvāmitra* thus gained an eternal place among the exalted sages.

I. Storytelling

Help King *Kauśika* become a *brahmarṣi* by telling his story. Form two teams. The teams alternate telling the story and the team which does the best storytelling wins the game.

Team 1

One day King *Kauśika* went to the forest with his army. There he met Sage *Vasiṣṭha*.............

Team 2

After being defeated, King *Kauśika* went to the south to do penance and became a *rājarṣi*. One day King *Triśaṅku*.............

Team 1

Rājarṣi Kauśika went to the west to do more penance. One day King *Hariścandra*'s son *Rohita* ....

Team 2

After great penance, Lord *Brahmā* made King *Kauśika* a *ṛṣi*.*Indra* sent *Menakā,* an *apsarā*.............

Team 1

Ṛṣi Kauśika then went to the north to do more penance and earned the title *maharṣi*. Then *Rambhā* was sent ....

Team 2

Finally, *Maharṣi Kauśika* went to the east for further penance and became ....

He also came to be known as *Viśvāmitra*.

II. Questions to Stimulate Discussion

1. Why was *Brahmarṣi Kauśika* known as *Viśvāmitra*?

2. Identify the different feelings that *Viśvāmitra* had to overcome in order to become a *brahmarṣi*.

STORY OF *ŚAKUNTALĀ*

Duṣyanta, a king in the lunar dynasty, one day went hunting with an entourage. Tired of wandering in the forest, *Duṣyanta* looked for a hermitage to rest and refresh himself. He came across Sage *Kaṇva's āśrama*. The sage was not in the hermitage at that time. As *Duṣyanta* entered the *āśrama*, he saw a beautiful maiden watering her favourite plants. *Duṣyanta*, enchanted by her beauty, fell in love with her. Relieved of his fatigue and captured by his desire for her, he asked her who she was and how she came to live in the forest. He concluded that since he, a *kṣatriya* king, felt so strongly for her, she must be the daughter of a *kṣatriya* alone.

Śakuntalā replied that she was the daughter of Sage *Viśvāmitra*, who had been a *kṣatriya* king, and *Menakā*. She added that Sage *Kaṇva* had raised her in his *āśrama* as his own daughter when *Menakā* abandoned her in the forest. *Śakuntalā* offered a seat to the king and extended all hospitality to him. *Śakuntalā* was also attracted towards the king. When *Duṣyanta* discovered this, he pointed out to her that a *kṣatriya* princess had the freedom to choose her own life-partner. *Śakuntalā* willingly accepted *Duṣyanta* and married him through *gāndharva-vivāha*. In the *gāndharva* system of marriage, the expression of mutual consent between the couple is sufficient to declare the couple as husband and wife. *Duṣyanta* spent the night with his bride *Śakuntalā* in the *āśrama* and returned to his capital the next day on an urgent mission.

Upon his return from his travels, the sage was pleased to know of *Śakuntalā's* marriage with *Duṣyanta*. Soon after, a son was born to *Śakuntalā*. The sage performed all the purificatory rites, *saṃskāras*, beginning with *jātakarma*, the birth ceremony, for the child. He was named *Sarvadamana*. He grew under the care of the sage and exhibited extraordinary valour. As a young lad, *Sarvadamana* fearlessly played with lion cubs in the forest and subdued them with his strength.

A long time lapsed and the king did not return from the capital. *Śakuntalā* became sad as she began to lose hope of *Duṣyanta* coming back. She went to the king's palace with her son. Anxious as she was to reunite with her husband, the king feigned ignorance about the marriage and did not accept the boy as his son.

A voice from the heaven declared that *Śakuntalā* was truly married to the king and the boy was, in fact, his son. The voice commanded the king to accept the boy as his son. From then on, the boy was called *Bharata*. *Duṣyanta* accepted *Śakuntalā* as his queen, and *Bharata* became the crown prince. After *Duṣyanta*, *Bharata* ruled his kingdom well and his country of rule was named after him as *Bhārata*.

Story of *Śakuntalā*

I. Fill in the blanks.

Complete the story by filling in the appropriate words.

Sarvadamana	*Kaṇva*	*Gāndharva-vivāha*
Śakuntalā	*Duṣyanta*	*Bharata*
Viśvāmitra	*Menakā*	pined
recognise	*Rambhā*	*Nārada*

1. *Śakuntalā* was born to _______________ and _______________.
2. Sage _______________ raised her in his hermitage.
3. King _______________ fell in love with *Śakuntalā*.
4. He married *Śakuntalā* through a form of marriage known as _______________.
5. *Śakuntalā* gave birth to _______________ in Sage *Kaṇva's* hermitage.
6. For a long time, *Śakuntalā* _______________ for King *Duṣyanta* to return.
7. King *Duṣyanta* did not _______________ her when she came to his palace.
8. On hearing the heavenly voice, he accepted _______________ and *Sarvadamana*.
9. *Sarvadamana* was known as _______________ from the time *Duṣyanta* accepted him.

II. Matching

Identify the relationships by drawing lines to connect the words.

	WHO?	RELATED TO WHOM?	HOW?
1.	Sage *Kaṇva*	*Menakā*	Husband
2.	*Duṣyanta*	*Śakuntalā*	Son
3.	*Bharata*	*Śakuntalā*	Foster-father
4.	*Śakuntalā*	*Duṣyanta*	Wife
5.	*Menakā*	*Viśvāmitra*	Daughter

STORY OF *SATĪ*

Dakṣa was a *mānasa-putra*, a mind-born son of Lord *Brahmā*, the creator. He was married to *Prasūti*, the third daughter of *Svāyambhuva Manu*. He had sixteen daughters, the youngest one being *Satī*. *Satī* married Lord *Śiva*.

Once *Prajāpati* performed a sacrifice known as *Brahma Satra* in which all sages and gods participated. *Dakṣa* also came to attend the sacrifice. Everyone in the assembly, except *Brahmā* and *Śiva*, stood up to honour *Dakṣa*, when *Dakṣa* entered. *Dakṣa* offered his salutation to his father *Brahmā* and took his seat. He noticed that *Śiva* neither stood up nor paid any attention to him.

Feeling insulted, *Dakṣa* abused *Śiva* in the assembly as one who was impure and ugly and accused him of indecent behaviour. He regretted that he gave his virtuous and beautiful daughter to an unworthy person based on the advice of his father. He proclaimed that *Śiva* would not get his share in the sacrificial offerings, *āhutis*, any more. *Śiva* distressed at the happenings, got up and returned to his abode with his *gaṇas*, attendants led by *Nandikeśvara*.

In course of time, *Brahmā* crowned *Dakṣa* as *Prajāpati*, the lord of created beings. *Dakṣa's* pride now grew manifold. Desiring to take revenge on *Śiva*, he once arranged to perform *Bṛhaspati Sava*, the greatest of all sacrifices. He invited all sages and gods along with their spouses except *Śiva*, his son-in-law.

Satī, his daughter, heard about her father's grand sacrifice. She saw a stream of women well-dressed and profusely decorated, proceeding towards the place of sacrifice along with their husbands. Prompted by a desire to witness the grand function that would be attended by all her affectionate sisters and their families, she went to her husband and entreated him for attending the sacrifice. She told him that even if an invitation was not received, they should not mind attending it, as a function at the place of *guru*, father or husband did not require an invitation.

Story of *Satī*

Story of *Satī* contd...

Śiva told her that it was not proper to visit a place uninvited where one would not be welcome. He revealed to her the insult meted out to him by *Dakṣa* in the assembly of gods and sages. But *Satī* was bent upon attending the function. In spite of *Śiva's* warning that she would not be received at her father's place, she proceeded alone.

As *Satī* reached the place of sacrifice, her father did not look at her. Fearing *Dakṣa*, none greeted her. She saw no oblation, *āhuti* was offered to her husband. *Satī* realised that *Dakṣa* had arranged the sacrifice only to take revenge on her husband. Hurt and angered, she ridiculed him for his prejudice against *Śiva* born out of pride of learning and power of penance and disowned him as her father. She sat in meditation and offered herself in the fire of *yoga* and brought an end to her form. The attendants of *Satī* rushed towards *Dakṣa* to kill him. *Bhṛgu*, the chief priest, invoked a *mantra* and created special beings known as *ribhus* to drive away the attendants and save the sacrifice.

Śiva came to know of the happenings in the sacrificial hall through Sage *Nārada*. Deciding to punish *Dakṣa*, he took out a strand of his matted locks and dashed it on the ground. A mighty being, known as *Vīrabhadra* arose from the strand and rushed to the spot of the sacrifice, as instructed by *Śiva*. Destroying the *yajña*, sacrifice, *Vīrabhadra* severed *Dakṣa's* head instantly. *Śiva* pardoned the sages who took part in the irregular *yajña*. At the request of *Brahmā*, he visited the *yajña-śālā* and blessed *Dakṣa* to regain his life. Freed of his pride, *Dakṣa* completed the sacrifice in the presence of *Śiva*. Praising the greatness of *Śiva*, *Dakṣa* ruled the beings for many *yugas*.

I. Storytelling

Form three teams. Each team will tell one part of *Satī's* story. The team which does the best storytelling wins the game. The story begins for each team as follows:

Team 1

During the *yajña*, all the *ṛṣis* stood up to honour *Dakṣa* except ....

Team 2

When *Satī* found out that her father was performing the *Bṛhaspati-sava*, she wanted to ....

Team 3

Śiva sent *Vīrabhadra* to destroy ....

II. Matching

Identify the relationships by drawing lines to connect the words.

	WHO?	RELATED TO WHOM?	HOW?
1.	*Dakṣa*	*Dakṣa*	Born of *mantra-śakti*
2.	*Ribhus*	*Śiva*	Father
3.	*Vīrabhadra*	*Bhṛgu*	Born of matted locks
4.	*Śiva*	*Śiva*	Father-in-law
5.	*Brahmā*	*Satī*	*Bhakta*
6.	*Nandi*	*Śiva*	Husband

III. Topics to Stimulate Discussion

Describe where these morals occur in *Satī's* story.

1. Arrogance is the seed of a great fall.

2. An adamant nature leads to self-destruction.

3. Worship without devotion is not accepted by the Lord.

STORY OF *MĀRKAṆḌEYA*

Sūta Maharṣi had been narrating the *Bhāgavata Purāṇa* to the sages headed by *Śaunaka* in *Naimiśaraṇya* forest. Towards the close of the narration, *Śaunaka* raised a doubt regarding Sage *Mārkaṇḍeya*. It was known that Sage *Mārkaṇḍeya* was born in the same *kalpa*, cycle of creation, as *Śaunaka*. The dissolution of the *kalpa* had not yet taken place. *Śaunaka* could not understand how Sage *Mārkaṇḍeya* could have the vision of the Lord in the form of a baby during the dissolution, as described in the *purāṇa*. *Śaunaka* asked for clarification. In reply, *Sūta Maharṣi* narrated the story of *Mārkaṇḍeya* as follows:

Mārkaṇḍeya was the son of Sage *Mṛkaṇḍu*. *Mṛkaṇḍu* initiated *Mārkaṇḍeya* into *Gāyatrī-mantra* with the *upanayana-saṃskāra*. Thus qualified to begin Vedic studies, *Mārkaṇḍeya* started learning the *Vedas* and *Vedāṅgas*. After duly completing his studies, he resolved to continue lifelong with the first stage of life, namely *brahmacarya*. Taking his abode in the *Himālayas*, he lived a life of penance. Thus when he was remaining absorbed in the thoughts of the Lord, many years rolled by.

Indra wanted to test the steadfastness of the sage. He sent beautiful celestial nymphs led by *Puñjikasthalā* to his hermitage but the sage remained undisturbed by them. Seeing their in-capacity to distract the sage and afraid of offending him, *Puñjikasthalā* retreated with her group. Lord *Nārāyaṇa* was pleased with the sage's mastery over his mind and senses. He came to the hermitage as sages *Nara* and *Nārāyaṇa*. *Mārkaṇḍeya* welcomed them with all devotion, as he knew they were Lord *Viṣṇc* himself. Pleased with *Mārkaṇḍeya*, they gave him a boon. *Mārkaṇḍeya* requested them to reveal the truth of *māyā*, because of which the diverse names and forms in the creation were perceived as real. *Nara* and *Nārāyaṇa* promised to reveal the truth soon and left for their abode in *Badarikāśrama*.

One day, *Mārkaṇḍeya* was absorbed in contemplation in his *āśrama* when he had a vision of dissolution of the creation. Heavy rains lashed on earth accompanied by strong winds, thunder and lightning. Soon there was water everywhere and the earth began to disappear under it. In the midst of the waters, he saw a beautiful baby full of effulgence, floating on a banyan leaf. The baby was holding the big toe of the right foot with his tiny hands into his mouth and sucking it. *Mārkaṇḍeya* went near the baby to have a close look, when he was sucked into the baby by its breath. Inside the baby, he saw the entire universe with mountains, rivers and oceans. He also saw his own *āśrama* inside the baby. Pushed out by the baby's exhalation, the sage again saw him out in the waters. In an instant, the baby vanished, the deluge disappeared and *Mārkaṇḍeya* was in his *āśrama* again.

Lord *Śiva* and *Pārvatī* met the sage and explained to him that the vision he had was the revelation of *māyā* shown by Lord *Nārāyaṇa* himself. The sage understood the *pralaya*, deluge, as one of the glories of *māyā* and realised that *māyā* was a mere appearance of names and forms effortlessly wielded by the Lord himself.

Story of *Mārkaṇḍeya*

I. Fill in the blanks.

Complete the story by filling in the appropriate words.

Vedas	planets	*apsarā*
devotee	boon	baby
vision	dissolution	universe

1. Sage *Mārkaṇḍeya* was an ascetic and had studied the ______________.
2. He was a great ______________ of the Lord.
3. *Indra* sent an ______________ to distract the sage, but was unsuccessful.
4. Sage *Mārkaṇḍeya* asked the Lord for a ______________.
5. One day, during the ______________ of the world, the sage saw waters tossed by winds and rains.
6. He saw a beautiful ______________ drifting in the waters.
7. The sage entered the baby's body and saw the entire ______________ inside him.
8. Sage *Mārkaṇḍeya* understood that he had been blessed by the ______________ of the Lord.

II. What do you learn from this story?

____

____

____

MATSYĀVATĀRA

In the eternal flow of time, one of the cycles of creation, namely a *kalpa*, was coming to its completion. This meant that Lord *Brahmā* would retire for the day, and during the night, the dissolution of the creation would take place. The tidal waves of the sea submerged the worlds under the waters. During that time, the demon *Hayagrīva*, the chief of the *asuras*, happened to be near *Brahmā*. He stole the *Vedas* coming out of Lord *Brahmā's* mouth and concealed them under the waters. Lord *Viṣṇu* saw this and decided to take the form of a fish to retrieve the *Vedas*.

In the same *kalpa*, there was a *rajarṣi*, a royal sage, who was a king as well as an ascetic, by the name *Satyavrata*. One day, *Satyavrata* was performing *jala-tarpaṇa*, oblations with water, on the banks of River *Kṛtamālā*. As he took the water from the river in his palms for the oblation, a tiny fish came with the water. He dropped the water back into the river in order to save its life. To the surprise of the king, the fish started speaking to him in human voice. It asked him to have compassion and not leave it in the river as its life was in danger because of bigger fishes. The merciful king agreed to protect the fish and dropped it in his *kamaṇḍalu*, a water-pot of coconut shell, and carried it to his *āśrama*.

By the next day, the fish had grown bigger. Finding the space in the *kamaṇḍalu* inadequate, the fish asked the king to provide a larger pot. The king did not observe anything unusual and gently placed it in a pitcher. In less than an hour, the fish grew bigger in size and appealed to the king to have mercy and provide a more spacious container of water. The king, containing his surprise, placed the fish in a pool of water. The fish instantly covered the space of the pond and again addressed the king. The king now saw this as an unusual phenomenon. He took the fish to the sea and placed it back in the sea water. He understood that the fish was none other than the Lord and offering his salutations, glorified him.

I. Unscramble the words.

1. *V Y A H G A Ī A R*
   The *asura* who stole the *Vedas* was

   __________________.

2. *V R T A Y Ā A S A T*
   There was a devoted king named

   __________________.

3. *Ā R H A M B*
   The creator is

   __________________.

4. *G S E S A*
   Holy men are called

   __________________.

5. *T M S A Y A*
   One incarnation of the Lord was

   __________________.

Matsyāvatāra contd...

The Lord then informed the king that on the seventh day hence, the dissolution of the creation would take place. He added that when the sea waters are about to submerge the worlds, a boat would be sent for him. The Lord instructed the king to board the ship and bring with him seeds of plants and herbs, as well as animals for the next creation. Seven great sages were also to accompany the king. The Lord advised the king to sail the boat undaunted by the tidal waves, as he would be guided in the darkness by the brilliance of the sages. The Lord added that he would appear on the waters as a giant fish with horns and the king should tie his boat to the horns of the fish. The Lord himself would guide the boat in the vast expanse of the waters until the completion of the night of *Brahmā*. The Lord assured *Satyavrata* that at that time he would bless him with his teachings.

Satyavrata felt happy and awaited the deluge of the worlds. The day arrived and the sea waters swelled with unprecedented rains submerging the land around. The earth began to disappear fast. *Satyavrata* saw a boat approaching him. He boarded it along with the seven sages. Singing praises of the Lord, they set the sail.

There was thick darkness all around, but the effulgence of the sages guided the boat on its sail. All of a sudden, a giant fish with horns and golden in colour appeared. King *Satyavrata* fastened the boat to the horns and guided by the Lord, guided them through the waters. Sporting in the waters, the Lord imparted the knowledge of truth to *Satyavrata*. The Lord also killed *Hayagrīva* and restored the *Vedas* to *Brahmā* at the dawn of the new day. The Lord, having completed his task as a fish, disappeared. *Satyavrata* became *Manu* in the next cycle of creation. He was known as *Vaivasvata Manu* and became the first being to propagate the human species.

II. Count Me

While crossing the ocean before the *Mahāpralaya*, King *Satyavrata* passed many things under the water. Count the items in the picture and indicate how many there are of each.

____ Octopus ____ Seahorses ____ Shells ____ Rocks____ Small Fish ____ Seaweeds ____ Starfish

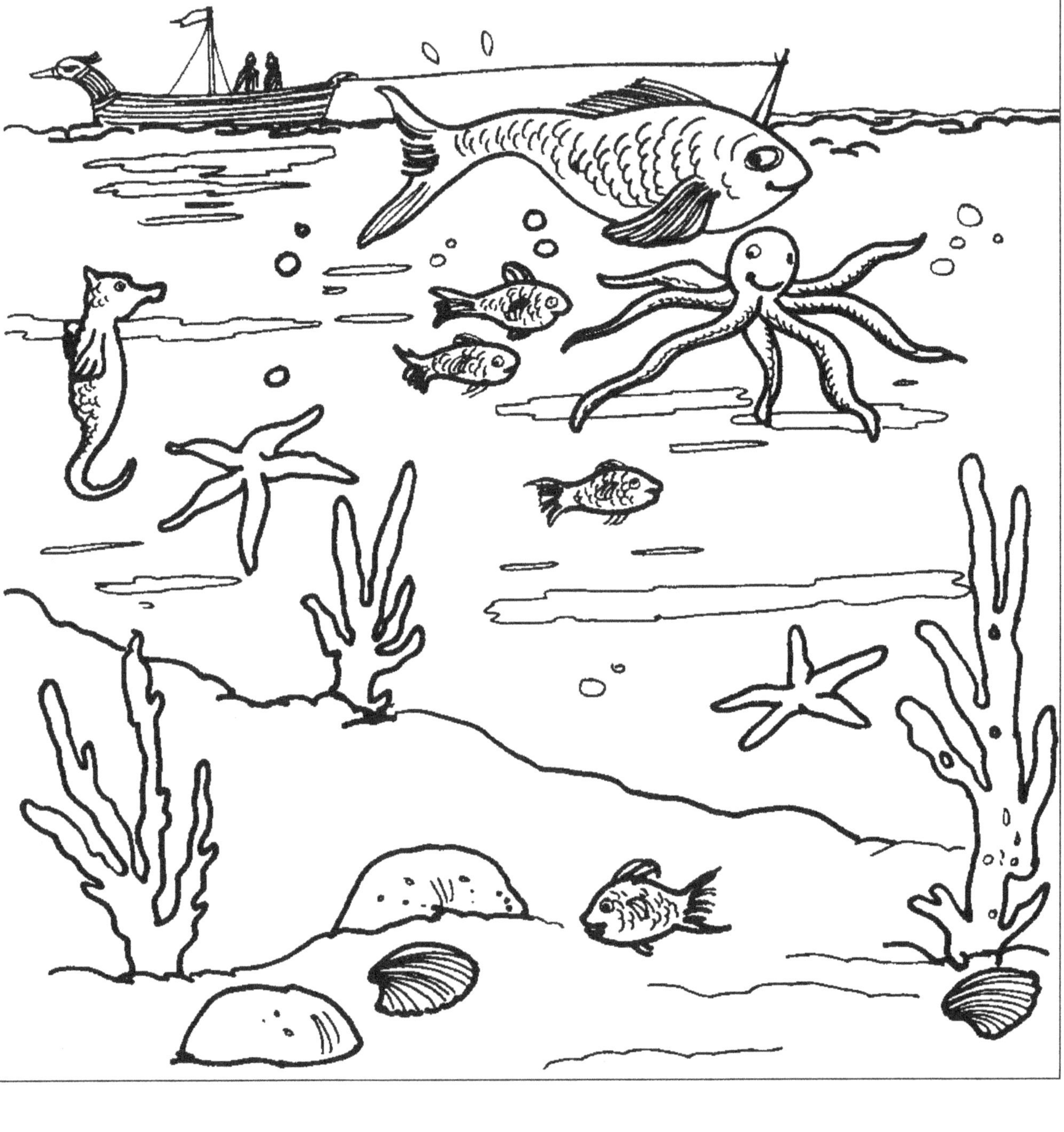

III. Fishing Game

Use the words floating around to fill in the blanks correctly.

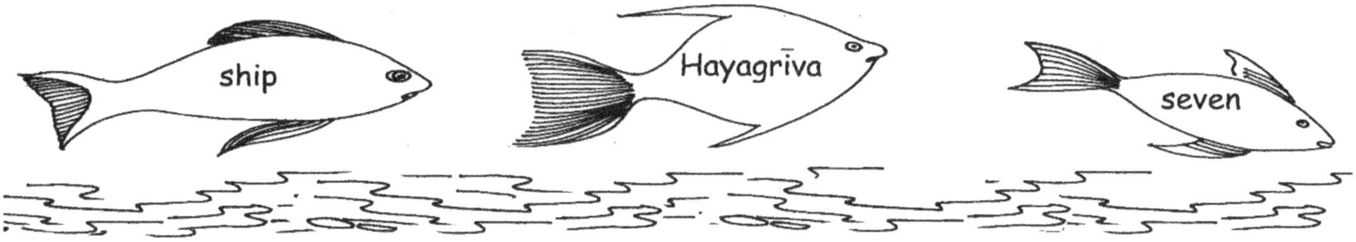

1) Lord *Viṣṇu* took the form of a ______________.

2) King *Satyavrata* took a ______________ with seeds and animals in it.

3) The king also took the ______________ sages.

4) A golden fish with a ______________ appeared.

5) It was Lord ______________ in His *Matsyāvatāra*.

6) The Lord killed the *asura* ______________.

7) Lord *Viṣṇu* gave the ______________ back to Lord *Brahmā*.

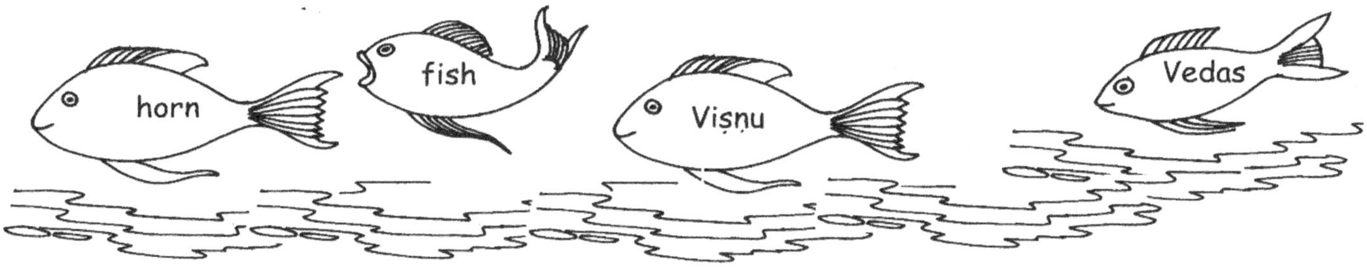

KŪRMĀVATĀRA

In the *Cākṣusa-manvantara*, the period of rule of *Cākṣusa Manu* and his descendants, the Lord manifested as *Kūrma*, a tortoise.

It so happened that once there was a fight between the *devas* and the *asuras* in the heavens. The *asuras* killed many *devas* and established supremacy over them. The Vedic sacrifices were not allowed to be performed on earth. *Indra*, the king of heavens; *Varuṇa*, the deity of waters; and other *devas* lost their splendour due to the absence of oblations from the sacrifices. Lacking the blessings of the *devatās*, the three worlds suffered. *Indra*, with other *devas*, approached Lord *Brahmā* for help. Lord *Brahmā* took them to the Milky Ocean, the abode of Lord *Viṣṇu* and praying fervently they sought Lord *Viṣṇu's* help. Pleased with their prayers, the Lord appeared before them and blessed them.

He suggested that they make peace with the powerful *asuras* and churn the Milky Ocean with their help. He assured them that they would receive nectar from the ocean as a result of churning, drinking which they would become immortal and overpower the *asuras* in future battles. He gave them detailed instructions as to how to go about this task, and advised them not to covet for any pleasurable objects that might emerge from the ocean during the churning. He also told them to avoid lashing out in anger against the *asuras* and not be afraid of the poison that might emerge from the ocean while churning. Offering salutations to the Lord, the *devas* returned to their abode.

Indra went to *Bali*, the chief of *asuras* and negotiated for peace. As the gain of nectar had to be accomplished, *Indra* did not mind the loss of honour in approaching *Bali* for help. He told *Bali* about the nectar and the need to churn the ocean together for the nectar, which could then be shared by all. *Bali* willingly agreed to the proposal.

As instructed by the Lord, the *devas* and *asuras* brought all the herbs and plants, and dropped them in the Milky Ocean. With the grace of the Lord, they carried Mount *Mandara* on *Garuḍa's* back to the ocean in order to use it as a churning rod. *Vāsuki*, the serpent king, agreed to be the cord for whirling the rod in the ocean as he was assured of his share of the nectar. Accordingly, they twined the long *Vāsuki* around the *Mandara* mountain. The Lord along with the *devas*, positioned himself near *Vāsuki's* head and the *devas* held the serpent in their hands. The *asuras* objected to holding the tail as they considered the tail inauspicious. The Lord expecting their objection and knowing what was in store for them near the head, welcomed the idea of switching sides. With the *devas* and the *asuras* ranging on either side of the *Mandara* rod and each pulling the ends of the coiled *Vāsuki* alternately, the churning began.

Kūrmāvatāra contd...

Soon after, in spite of holding the cord tightly during the churning, due to its weight the *Mandara* mountain sank in the waters. The Lord knew that this was because they had not invoked Lord *Vigneśvara* before starting the endeavour. He took the form of huge tortoise and went under the waters. He bore the mountain on his back and arose. The *devas* and the *asuras* rejoiced at the sight of the mountain again. The Lord, in the form of the tortoise, continued to support the mountain on his back and the churning began once again.

As *Vāsuki* was being pulled on both sides in great velocity and force, he began to emit fire and poisonous smoke. Having taken their position near *Vāsuki's* head, the *asuras* suffered the heat and fumes and were unable to proceed with the churning. The Lord took over the churning on both the sides. Soon after, the deadly poison, *hālāhala*, also known as *kālakūṭa*, emerged from the surface of the ocean. Frightened at the mere sight of the poison, the *devas* rushed to Lord *Śiva* for protection. Lord *Śiva* swallowed the poison and thus protected everyone.

The poison had been the consolidated impurities of the ocean. Now that the impurities had been consumed by the Lord, as the churning continued, there arose many beautiful things from the ocean. The divine *Kāmadhenu* appeared first and was gifted to the sages headed by *Vasiṣṭha* for the performance of their daily rituals. Then came the beautiful horse *Uccaiśravas* which was taken by *Bali*. The majestic elephant *Airāvata* with four tusks followed and was given to *Indra*. The Lord took the jewel *Kaustubha* that arose from the ocean.

The wish-fulfilling *Pārijāta* tree and women with captivating beauty, the *apsarās*, were presented to the heavens. Goddess *Lakṣmī*, in all her grace and splendour appeared before all. Everyone desired her, wanting her for them-selves. But she chose Lord *Viṣṇu* and married him.

I. Fill in the blanks.

Complete the story with the appropriate words.

Bali	mount *Mandara*	*Rāma*
devas	*Rāvaṇa*	*asuras*
Vigneṣvara	*kūrma*	snake

1. The _______________ and _______________ fought many wars in the heavens.

2. To churn the ocean the *devas* used the _______________ as a churning staff.

3. The _______________ *Vāsuki* was the churning rope.

4. The Lord incarnated as a _______________ to hold the mountain on his back.

5. *Indra* went to as _______________, the chief of *asuras* and negotiated for peace.

6. Mt. *Mandara* sank in the water because they had forgotten to pray to Lord_______________.

II. Find Me

The churning of the ocean offered the devas and asuras six items. Identify and colour them.

Kūrmāvatāra contd...

The churning went on. Finally, Lord *Dhanvantari* arose with a golden pot containing the nectar. He was none other than Lord *Nārāyaṇa* himself. The *asuras* snatched the pot from him and began fighting among themselves as to who should consume the nectar first. The *devas* sought help from the Lord, and all of a sudden, a beautiful woman *Mohinī*, appeared. The *asuras*, captivated by her charms and appearance, sought her intervention in the distri-bution of the nectar. *Mohinī* agreed to the request on a condition that they would accept whichever way she chose to distribute the nectar. The *asuras*, in their delusion, willingly agreed to her condition and gave her the pot of nectar.

Mohinī asked the *asuras* and the *devas* to sit in a row. With her charming movements and speech, she mesmerised the *asuras* and went about distributing the nectar to the *devas*. One *asura* quietly took a seat in between the sun deity and the moon deity, and partook the nectar. Realising what had happened, the Lord chopped off the head of the *asura* with his disc. The head remained immortal due to the prior consumption of the nectar, while the tail fell dead. The Lord honoured the head, by making him a planet called *Rāhu*. Thus partaking the nectar, the *devas* became very powerful and vanquishing the *asuras* in a battle, regained their supremacy and splendour.

III. Crossword Puzzle

Identify the items that emerged during the churning of the ocean.

ACROSS

1. Her milk was used for Vedic rituals.
2. It was swallowed by Lord *Śiva*.
3. She married Lord *Nārāyaṇa*.
4. The tusker that was given to *Indra*.
5. *Bali* took this white animal.

DOWN

6. She charmed the *asuras*.
7. He carried the nectar.
8. The Lord wore it as an ornament.
9. It was known as the *Pārijāta*.

VARĀHĀVATĀRA

At the beginning of creation, *Svāyambhuva Manu* and *Śatarūpā* emerged from *Brahmā*. *Satarūpā* became *Svāyambhuva Manu's* wife and had two sons, namely, *Priyavrata* and *Uttānapāda*, and three daughters, namely, *Ākūti*, *Devahūti* and *Prasūti*.

Having initiated the propagation of human species, *Brahmā* commanded *Svāyambhuva Manu* to rule the earth righteously. He asked *Manu* to live a life with devotion towards the Lord and worship him through Vedic sacrifices. *Svāyambhuva Manu* sought an abode for himself and his progeny in order to carry out his duties. At that time, the earth was submerged in the waters due to the previous dissolution of the creation.

As *Brahmā* reflected upon how to recover the earth from the waters, there appeared in the sky a tiny boar, which instantly grew to an alarming size. *Brahmā* and others wondered at the weird looking creature and began to speculate about its identity. The loud roar of the boar resounding in all the quarters, made it obvious that the boar was none other than the Lord himself. *Brahmā* offered his salutations to the Lord and sang hymns in praise of him.

The divine boar, Lord *Varāha*, then dived deep into the waters and reached the bottom of the ocean. Sniffing through the waters, Lord *Varāha* discovered the earth and lifted it on its white tusks. As the Lord began to rise from the ocean bed towards the surface of the ocean, *Nārada* informed the demon *Hiraṇyākṣa*, regarding the whereabouts of the Lord.

Hiraṇyākṣa was the son of Sage *Kaśyapa* and *Diti*. He and his brother, *Hiraṇyakaśipu*, were conceived by *Diti* at a time that was inappropriate for union, as it was *pradoṣa-kāla*, the time for worship of the Lord. The two sons born to *Diti* from that union turned out to be *asuras*. *Hiraṇyākṣa* was so proud of his powers that he wanted to have a battle with the Lord and defeat him.

I. Help Me

Help Lord *Varāha* find the surface of the sea to re-establish Mother Earth.

Varāhāvatāra contd...

There is an interesting story that describes the cause of *Hiraṇyākṣa's* birth. Once, the sages *Sanaka* and his three brothers went to *Vaikuṇṭha* to meet Lord *Viṣṇu*. They passed through many entrance gates, and when they reached the seventh entrance, they did not take notice of the two young *dvārapālakas*, guards, standing with mace in their hands. The guards were offended and stopped them on their way. Thus provoked, the sages got angry at the guards and pronounced a curse on them for their arrogance. The sages cursed them to be born as *asuras* on earth. The guards, *Jaya* and *Vijaya*, realised their folly and expressed their apology to the sages.

Lord *Viṣṇu* came to know of the insult suffered by his attendants, who happened to be his devotees, and came to their aid. He told them that they would have only three births after which they would return to *Vaikuṇṭha*. He added that in all the three births, they would meet their end in the hands of the Lord alone. In their first birth, *Jaya* and *Vijaya* were born as *Hiraṇyakaśipu* and *Hiraṇyākṣa*. This was followed by their second birth in which they were *Rāvaṇa* and *Kumbhakarṇa*. They completed their curse with the final birth in which they were *Śiśupāla* and *Dantavaktra*.

As soon as *Hiraṇyākṣa* found out that the Lord was inside the ocean waters in the form of a boar, he went in and obstructed the Lord's way in the waters. Confronting him, Lord *Varāha* reached the surface of the waters and placed the earth on the surface. A fight ensued between him and the *asura* in which Lord *Varāha* destroyed *Hiraṇyākṣa* with his *Sudarśana-cakra*.

The *devas* rejoiced at the fall of the *asura* and *Brahmā* offered his prayers extolling the Lord's glories. Having got the earth as his abode, *Svāyambhuva Manu* propagated the human species and ruled the earth gloriously.

II. Fill in the blanks.

Complete the story with the appropriate words.

creation	tusk	sword	*Hiraṇyākṣa*
lion	Earth	boar	*Mahābali*

1. Lord incarnated as *Varāha* to retrieve Mother ____________ submerged under the waters.

2. Lord *Viṣṇu*, as a _______________, jumped into the deep waters.

3. There he fought the *rākṣasa* named _______________.

4. He lifted Mother Earth on his _______________ and saved her.

5. Thus the process of _______________ continued uninterrupted.

III. Mark it with an X.

Mark the "odd one out" (the one that does not belong in the group).

Group 1

_____ *Jaya* _____ *Vijaya* _____ *Hiraṇykaśipu*

_____ Snake _____ *Hiraṇyākṣa*

Group 2

_____ Water _____ Earth _____ Sky

_____ Fire _____ Map

Group 3

_____ Boar _____ Grunt _____ *Avatāra*

_____ Tusk _____ Fish

Group 4

_____ Arrogant _____ Unrighteous _____ Selfish

_____ Compassionate _____ Destructive

Group 5

_____ Creation _____ Sustenance

_____ Dissolution _____ Damage

NARASIMHĀVATĀRA

Hiraṇyākṣa and *Hiraṇyakaśipu* were the two *asuras* born to Sage *Kaśyapa* and *Diti*. *Hiraṇyākṣa* was slain by the Lord in his manifestation as *Varāha*, boar. *Hiraṇyakaśipu* was very angry at the killing of his beloved brother. He vowed to avenge his brother's death and sever the head of his killer. He summoned his ministers and commanded them to destroy the righteous people and the places of sacrifices, so that Lord *Nārāyaṇa*would not get any oblation. The demons began to carry out the commands of their chief. They harassed the righteous people and burnt down the places of sacrifices. *Adharma* became rampant everywhere. The dharmic people began to fear for their lives.

Hiraṇyakaśipu desired to have undisputed lordship of all the three worlds. He decided to practise severe penance in order to win the grace of Lord *Brahmā*, and went to a valley of Mount *Mandara* for this purpose. Pleased with his austerities, *Brahmā* appeared before *Hiraṇyakaśipu* and offered him a boon.

Hiraṇyakaśipu asked for a boon whereby he would not be killed by any being created by *Brahmā* or any one else. He did not want his death to occur either inside or outside, either in the day or in the night. He added that no weapons should cause his death, either on earth or in space, and finally he sought undisputed lordship over all beings. The lord granted all his boons and blessed him. Convinced that he was the most exalted in the entire creation, *Hiraṇyakaśipu* went about fearlessly doing everything he wanted to do; people suffered under the tyranny of his rule.

One day when *Hiraṇyakaśipu* was performing his penance, the *devas* attacked the *asuras*. *Indra* captured *Hiraṇyakaśipu's* pregnant wife, *Kayādhū* and carried her away in order to kill the *asura* child in her womb.

Narasiṃhāvatāra contd...

Sage *Nārada* revealed to *Indra* that the baby in the womb was a devotee of Lord *Nārāyaṇa* and releasing her from *Indra*, took her to his *āśrama*. *Kayādhū* served the sage with devotion. *Nārada* used to narrate the glories of Lord *Nārāyaṇa* to her and the child in the womb also used to listen to the teachings. When *Hiraṇyakaśipu* returned from his penance, *Nārada* sent *Kayādhū* back to her husband's place and soon after she gave birth to *Prahlāda*.

Prahlāda was born as a devotee of Lord *Nārāyaṇa*. He exhibited all virtues in him unlike the people of his race. He remained absorbed in the thoughts of the Lord chanting his name or singing his glories. *Hiraṇyakaśipu* appointed *Śaṇḍa* and *Amarka*, the two sons of his *Guru Śukrācārya* as teachers for *Prahlāda* and asked them to teach him texts dealing with the pursuits of *artha*, money and power and *kāma*, pleasures of life.

One day, *Hiraṇyakaśipu* called the five year old *Prahlāda* and asked him to summarise all that he had learnt. *Prahlāda* replied that surrender to Lord *Nārāyaṇa* was the only means for liberation from the sufferings of human life. *Hiraṇyakaśipu* was shocked to hear this. To prevent the influence of the devotees of Lord *Nārāyaṇa*, he sent the boy to the teachers' residence where he was asked to live and study.

Prahlāda continued to talk words of wisdom and show his devotion for Lord *Nārāyaṇa*. *Śaṇḍa* and *Amarka* tried their best to make him learn things that would please the king. But they could not change *Prahlāda's* mind. *Prahlāda* returned home but much to *Hiraṇyakaśipu's* discontent continued to talk about the glories of the Lord.

Hiraṇyakaśipu developed hatred for *Prahlāda* and ordered his killing. His people used various methods to kill *Prahlāda* but they were unsuccessful. The weapons used against him became blunted. Wild elephants trampled on him without any impact. He was hurled down from the top of a peak, and he got up as if nothing had happened. Poisonous snakes could not bite him to death. Blazing fire could not burn even the hair on his body. He was buried alive under the earth, but he continued to live. Frustrated with the failure of all his efforts, *Hiraṇyakaśipu* sent him back to his teachers' place.

I. Find Me

Identify four items shown below that were used to kill *Prahlāda* and colour them.

Narasiṃhāvatāra contd...

Once when the teachers were away, *Prahlāda* revealed to his co-students how he had listened to the glories of the Lord from Sage *Nārada* while in his mother's womb. He, then, taught them everything he had learnt from the sage. The teachers came to know about *Prahlāda's* influence on the minds of other children. Annoyed, they informed *Hiraṇyakaśipu* and sent him back home.

Hiraṇyakaśipu decided that he himself would put an end to *Prahlāda's* life. He sent for him. *Prahlāda* came and stood calmly before his father who was filled with rage. *Hiraṇyakaśipu* ruthlessly told him of his intention, but *Prahlāda* only felt sorry for him and asked him again to accept Lord *Nārāyaṇa* as the most powerful. He pointed out how his father's own wrong thinking was his worst enemy, not Lord *Nārāyaṇa. Hiraṇyakaśipu* retorted asking *Prahlāda* to show him the place of existence of Lord *Nārāyaṇa.* He wanted to know why the Lord was not visible in the facing pillar if he truly existed everywhere. He threatened to sever *Prahlāda's* head and challenged the Lord to protect him. So saying, *Hiraṇyakaśipu* went towards the pillar with a sword in his hand and hit the pillar with his fist.

At that moment, the pillar split with a thunderous noise and the Lord emerged in a terrifying form as *Narasiṃha,* lion-faced human being. *Hiraṇyakaśipu* rushed towards the Lord. *Narasiṃha* pounced upon him and carried him to the threshold. It was the twilight hour. Keeping *Hiraṇyakaśipu* on his lap, the Lord tore open his chest with his claws and roared. While the celestials rejoiced at the fall of the mighty demon, none dared to look at or approach *Narasiṃha* who was in full fury due to the offence caused by the demon towards his devotee.

Young *Prahlāda* was asked to pacify the Lord. *Prahlāda* approached him and offered his salutations. The Lord blessed him. *Prahlāda* sang the glories of the Lord, his voice choking with emotions and his eyes shedding tears of joy. The Lord bestowed a long life to *Prahlāda* lasting upto the end of the *kalpa* and offered him all pleasures of the world during his life-time.

II.Complete the Boon

III. Word Search

Find the following words, which appear up, down, across and diagonally in the word game.

Hiraṇyakaśipu	Lord	snake	fire	prayer
Nārāyaṇa	*asura*	poison	elephant	pillar

H	R	S	H	N	P	S	T	R	M	O	N	Y
P	I	L	L	A	R	N	T	G	U	P	U	B
Q	S	R	N	X	R	A	D	A	N	R	M	I
W	E	R	A	D	I	K	R	U	M	A	I	M
R	T	E	V	Ṇ	E	E	O	A	P	Y	S	B
T	B	S	W	O	Y	S	L	E	M	E	I	C
M	N	Ā	R	Ā	Y	A	Ṇ	A	N	R	S	G
N	T	G	N	J	Y	R	K	S	E	O	V	V
S	O	S	W	A	S	U	R	A	M	B	L	T
H	O	S	M	W	A	B	P	E	Ś	M	F	Y
V	T	E	I	N	M	W	I	S	D	I	O	U
O	F	G	W	O	M	R	S	S	R	O	P	T
E	T	N	A	H	P	E	L	E	T	M	O	U

VĀMANĀVATĀRA

Indra and other *devas* had regained their glory after acquiring the nectar from the churning of the Milky Ocean. *Bali*, the *asura* chief, had been vanquished by *Indra* in a fight. *Śukrācārya*, the *guru* of the *asura* clan, however, had intervened and saved *Bali's* life.

Bali was grateful to the sages of the *Bhṛgu* race, *Śukrācārya* and his descendants. He served them with devotion and offered them rich tributes. He sought guidance from *Śukrācārya* for regaining the kingdom of heavens. *Śukrācārya* assured *Bali* of success and performed a symbolic coronation ceremony for him. He asked *Bali* to perform the *Viśvajit* sacrifice, in which one gives one's entire wealth in charity in order to conquer the heavens. When the ritual was nearing completion, a beautiful chariot arose from the fire altar containing an armour, a bow and arrows which were received by *Bali*. *Bali's* grandfather, *Prahlāda*, came and presented him a garland that would never fade; and *Śukrācārya* presented him a conch. *Bali* was thus blessed by all.

Mounting on the divine chariot and equipped with the armour and bow, *Bali* marched to *Amrāvati* the capital of *Indra*, with his army. He blew the conch at the gates of the city and instilled fear in the hearts of the *devas*. Seeing the army led by the invincible *Bali*, *Indra* approached his *guru Bṛhaspati* for advice. *Bṛhaspati* told *Indra* of the help provided by *Śukrācārya* to *Bali* and advised him to go into hiding for some time. He said that *Bali* would meet his downfall by his own deed of insult to his *guru*, who was now instrumental in his success. *Indra* and other *devas* fled from the heavens. *Bali* occupied the throne of *Amarāvati* without any resistance and brought the three worlds under his command.

Aditi, mother of *devas*, was distressed at the disappearance of her sons. She narrated her sufferings to Sage *Kaśyapa*, her husband on his return from his travels. She asked him to suggest a way for the *devas* to retrieve their lost glory.

Kaśyapa replied that if she worshipped the Lord through the discipline of *payovrata*, a discipline in which one lives on milk alone, Lord *Viṣṇu* would fulfill her desires. He instructed her on the method of worship, which involved worshipping the Lord for twelve days in the bright fortnight of the month of *Phālguna*. The vow had to be observed from *Amāvāsyā*, New Moon day, when one offered prayers to Mother Earth and Lord *Viṣṇu* after taking a religious bath. A special *pūjā* had to be performed, chanting the twelve syllabled *mantra* - "*oṃ namo bhagavate vāsudevāya*" - salutation unto Lord *Vāsudeva*.

The next day one had to begin taking only milk diet, observe total silence, sleep on the ground, bathe three times a day and abstain from worldly enjoyments. One had to perform one's daily religious duties with the *vrata*, vow. For twelve days one had to thus live a life of worship and contemplation. On the thirteenth day, the *vrata* would be completed with special *pūjās* and feeding of the sattvic people and offering of *dakṣiṇā* and charities.

I. A Pot of Puzzles

Complete this puzzle by using the clues given below.

Line 1	*Aditi* was the *deva*'s __________
Line 2	The *asura* king
Line 3	A teacher is also called
Line 4	*Vāmana*'s father
Line 5	The *yajña* that *Bali* performed
Line 6	Thread ceremony
Line 7	*Bali* conquered this *loka*
Line 8	An *avatāra*
Line 9	Lord of *deva*'s
Line 10	*Bali* was their king

Vāmanāvatāra contd...

Aditi observed the *payovrata* in all earnestness and followed the injunctions to every detail. Finally, the Lord appeared before her. At the sight of the Lord, her joy knew no bounds and she extolled him with words of praise. The Lord promised to fulfill her desire and told her that he would be born to her soon for this purpose.

On the twelfth day of the bright fortnight of the lunar month of *Bhādrapada*, the Lord took birth at noon. He grew to the size of a dwarf, *vāmana*. He was known as *Upendra*, brother of *Indra*, as he was born to *Aditi*, *Indra's* mother. The sage performed the *upanayana-saṃskāra* for *Vāmana*. *Bṛhaspati* placed the sacred thread across his shoulder, while *Kaśyapa* tied the waist-cord made of *muñja* grass. Mother Earth gave him the deer skin seat and the moon deity presented the sacred staff. Mother *Aditi* dressed him with the loin-cloth and *Brahmā* blessed him with a *kamaṇḍalu*, water-pot. Goddess *Sarasvatī* offered him a rosary made of *akṣa* beeds. *Kubera*, the deity of wealth, gave the *bhikṣā-pātra*, the vessel to collect alms, while *Parvatī Devī* gave him the first *bhikṣā*. Thus honoured by all the assembled gods, goddesses and sages, *Vāmana* was initiated and carried the lustre of *brahma-tejas*, a brilliance that one acquires only after the completion of Vedic studies.

Vāmana once heard that *Bali* was performing the *Aśvamedha* sacrifice in *Bhṛgukaccha* on the northern banks of River *Narmadā*. He walked towards the sacrificial place holding his tiny umbrella and staff in one hand and the *kamaṇḍalu* in the other. As he reached the entrance of the *yajña-śālā*, the sacrificial hall, the priests led by *Śukrācārya*, welcomed him. They were struck in awe at the effulgence on the face of the young boy. *Bali* greeted him with honours due to a *brāhmaṇa*. Expressing his joy at the arrival of the brahmin boy, *Bali* asked him what he could do for him. The king offered him many gifts in the form of houses, cattle and other wealth.

Vāmana smiled and replied that *Bali's* words reflected his character of truthfulness and generosity. He reminded him of the glories of his ancestors who were magnanimous and always fulfilled their promises. Glorifying *Bali* and his ancestors, *Vāmana* asked *Bali* for three paces of land as measured by his feet. The Lord continued saying that by asking anything more than this, he would incur sin as that would mean exceeding his requirements. *Bali* promised to give the land measured by three footsteps.

II. Find Me

What is the boon that the young brahmin asked of King Bali? Identify and colour.

Vāmanāvatāra contd...

As *Bali* took his *kamaṇḍalu* to offer water in making a solemn vow to gift the promised land, his *guru*, *Śukrācārya* warned *Bali* that *Vāmana* was Lord *Viṣṇu* himself who had come to deprive *Bali* of everything that he had. *Bali*, having promised *Vāmana*, did not want to retract his promise and was ready to face the consequence. He politely rejected the advice of his *guru*. *Śukrācārya* became angry at *Bali's* disobedience and cursed him his downfall. *Bali* did not swerve from his promise and went ahead to gift the land sought by *Vāmana*.

All of a sudden, *Vāmana* began to grow in size until he had covered the entire creation. Stunned at this phenomenon, *Bali* and others saw the cosmic form of the Lord in which the entire universe was contained. They saw the earth, the intermediary space, mountains, rivers, oceans and all living beings.

The Lord, with his first stride, measured the entire earth that belonged to *Bali*. As he took his second stride, he covered the region upto *Brahmaloka*, the abode of *Brahmā*. *Brahmā* and the other sages were joyous to see the approaching feet of the Lord. They washed his feet with water and worshipped them. The water that fell from the feet of the Lord flew in the heavens as *Mandākinī* also known as *Ākāśa Gaṅgā*. There was no more space left for the Lord to measure his third pace. He stood before *Bali* again as a *Vāmana*. *Garuḍa*, the divine Eagle, bound *Bali* with *Varuṇa-pāśa*, cords of *Varuṇa*, and held him as a prisoner before *Vāmana*.

The Lord pointed out to *Bali* that he had not fulfilled his promise as the third pace of land remained to be claimed by him. *Bali*, committed to his pledge, offered his head for the Lord, to place his third step. *Bali* added that the last step had truly turned out to be a blessing for him as the Lord had taken away his pride and arrogance. Pleased with him, the Lord released *Bali* from his bondage of worldly existence. The Lord praised him for his steadfastness to truth even at the time of losing his wealth by the Lord's first step; his honour, when he was bound by *Garuḍa*; his *guru*, when he cursed *Bali*; and the kinsmen, who abandoned him when he lost everything. The Lord blessed *Bali* to be the *Manu* in the following *Manvantara* known as *Sāvarṇi*. *Bali* shed tears of joy and with gratitude, offered his salutations to the Lord.

III. Unscramble the words.

1. U G Y O N

   The radiant *Vāmana* was ______________.

2. B L U R E L M A

   In one hand, *Vāmana* carried an ______________.

3. O L B W

   In the other hand, *Vāmana* carried a ______________.

4. E U H G

   Vāmana suddenly grew to be ______________.

5. I B L A

   Vāmana blessed King ______________.

IV. Story Writing

Complete this story by using sentences from below.

I. 1. *Vāmana* went to meet King *Bali*.

2. ______________________________

3. *Bali* wanted to give *Vāmana* many gifts.

4. ______________________________

5. But *Vāmana* only wanted three steps of land.

6. ______________________________

7. His first two steps covered the earth and heaven.

8. ______________________________

Sentences to fill in:

i) The king offered *Vāmana* horses, cattle & wealth. ii) *Vāmana* grew in size and covered the earth. iii) The Lord kept his third step on king *Bali*'s head. iv) King *Bali* welcomed the young boy.

II. If you were given three boons what would you ask for and why?

1. ______________________________

____

2. ______________________________

____

3. ______________________________

____

PARAŚURĀMĀVATĀRA

Paraśurāma is held in the tradition as an incarnation of Lord *Viṣṇu*, taken by the Lord for the purpose of punishing the unrighteous *Haihaya* rulers of the *kṣatriya* race. The *kṣatriyas* were supposed to protect the sattvic people. Instead, they killed Sage *Jamadagni* and derelicted from their duty.

At the time of *Paraśurāma*, the youngest son of Sage *Jamadagni* and *Reṇukā*, *Kārtavīryārjuna* was the ruler of the kingdom of *Haihaya*. *Māhiṣmatī* was his capital. He worshipped Lord *Dattātreya* and obtained many boons such as having one thousand arms and extraordinary powers including a capacity to assume an atom-like minute form, and a capacity to travel all over the three worlds just as wind. *Kārtavīryārjuna* thus enjoyed unrivalled glory and affluence.

Once, when he was sporting in the waters of River *Narmadā*, *Kārtavīryārjuna* playfully stopped the flow of the river with his thousand arms. This caused inundation of *Rāvaṇa's* military camp nearby. Annoyed, *Rāvaṇa* rushed to *Kārtavīryārjuna* and insulted him. But *Kārtavīryārjuna's* prowess was so great that he effortlessly caught hold of *Rāvaṇa* and kept him in custody for some time before letting him go.

One day, *Kārtavīryārjuna* went on a hunt. He happened to come across Sage *Jamadagni's* hermitage. The sage had a divine cow, *Kāmadhenu*, with whose grace, he extended all hospitality to the king and his army. *Kārtavīryārjuna* became extremely jealous of *Jamadagni's* divine possession, and desiring the same, he ordered his men to take away the cow. The king then returned to his capital.

Paraśurāma who was away at that time returned after a while, and heard of the unrighteous act of the king. Raging with anger, he took his axe and bow and rushed to *Māhiṣmatī*. *Kārtavīryārjuna* saw *Paraśurāma* entering the city with the fury of a lion.

Story of *Paraśurāma*

I. Vowel Game

The printing machine is not printing the letters a, e, i, o, u properly. Fill in these alphabets correctly and complete this story.

K_ng K_rt_v_ry_rj_n_ c__ld

b_c_m_ _s sm_ll _s _n _t_m

_nd tr_v_l _ll _v_r th_ w_rld.

H_ w_nt_d th_ d_v_n_ c_w.

B_t S_g_ J_m_d_gn_ w__ld

n_t g_v_ K_m_dh_n_.

S_ th_ k_ng _rd_r_d

h_s m_n t_ t_k_ th_

c_w _w_y.

He sent an army of seventeen *akṣauhiṇīs*, battalions to fight him. *Paraśurāma* destroyed all of them. *Kārtavīryārjuna* himself faced *Paraśurāma* with his bows and arrows. Making use of his thousand arms he sent a rain of arrows at *Paraśurāma*. After an intense battle, *Paraśurāma* chopped his arms and head with his axe, and retrieved the divine cow.

On his return, he narrated his heroic deed to his father *Jamadagni*. But the sage disapproved of his action. He told him that he had committed a grave mistake by killing the king, as patience and forgiveness alone were the *dharma* of a *brāhmaṇa*. He added that in order to atone for his wrong action *Paraśurāma* should visit the holy places and bathe in the sacred rivers. *Paraśurāma* obeyed his father and went on a pilgrimage for one year.

The sons of *Kārtavīryārjuna* decided to avenge the death of their father. They had been waiting for an opportunity to visit the *āśrama* deceitfully and kill *Paraśurāma's* father when he was alone. One day, *Paraśurāma* went to the forest with his brothers to collect twigs for the daily rituals. *Kārtavīryārjuna's* sons entered the hermitage when the sage was in meditation, cut off his head and fled with it. Hearing *Reṇukā's* loud cry, *Paraśurāma* rushed back to the *āśrama*. In an outburst of grief at the death of his father and of indignation for the cruel act of *Kārtavīryārjuna's* sons, *Paraśurāma* resolved to wipe out the *kṣatriya* race from the earth for their adharmic actions.

He went to *Māhiṣmatī* and killed all the sons of *Kārtavīryārjuna*. Then going around the earth twentyone times, *Paraśurāma* almost totally wiped out the *kṣatriya* race. He, then, brought back the head of his father and joining it with his body, performed the last rites. *Jamadagni*, redeemed by the rituals of *Paraśurāma*, became one of the seven sages who eternally adorn the sky.

Paraśurāma finally went to Mount *Mahendra* where he spent the remaining part of his human life in austerities and penance.

II. My Thoughts

Draw your picture or stick your photo at the centre. Now complete these thought bubbles.

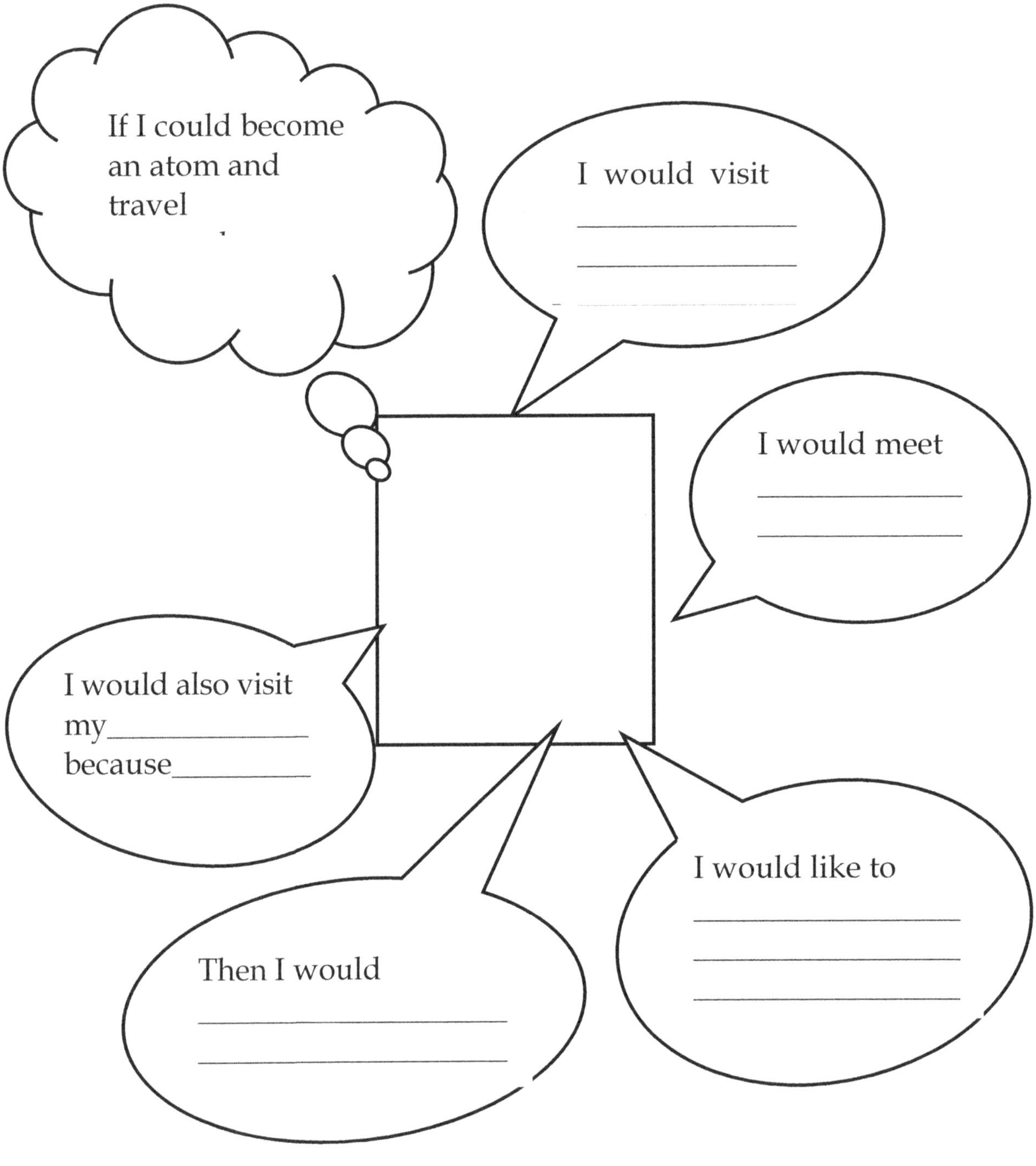

If I could become an atom and travel
I would visit
I would meet
I would also visit my
because
Then I would
I would like to

III. Fill in the blanks.

Complete the story by filling in the appropriate words.

Paraśurāma	*Jamadagni*	*Reṇukā*	good
unrighteous	*Kāmadhenu*	*Māhiṣmatī*	all

1. *Paraśurāma* was the son of Sage _______________ and _____________.

2. _______________ was the capital city of King *Kārtavīryārjuna.*

3. King *Kārtavīryārjuna* stole the cow named _______________.

4. The king's sons killed _______________'*s* father.

5. *Paraśurāma* destroyed _______________ the _______________ *kṣatriyas.*

RĀMĀVATĀRA

Lord *Rāma* was born in the solar dynasty and was known as *Raghukula Tilaka*, the foremost among the descendants of *Raghu*.

Daśaratha, *Raghu's* grandson, ruled the kingdom of *Kosala* from the capital of *Ayodhyā*. He had three queens, *Kausalyā*, *Sumitrā* and *Kaikeyī*. But his heart was sorrowful as he had no progeny. He arranged to perform the *putrakāmeṣṭi*, a ritual for begetting children. All the *devatās* assembled at the *yajña-śālā* to receive their oblations in the *yajña*. Seeing that the time was opportune, they prayed to Lord *Viṣṇu* for relief from the harassments of *Rāvaṇa*, the powerful *rākṣasa* king of *Laṅkā*. The Lord blessed them and assured them that he would be born as *Daśaratha's* son and would kill *Rāvaṇa*.

As the ritual was about to end, a divine being appeared from the fire altar with a pot of *pāyasam*, sweetened rice with milk, and asked *Daśaratha* to distribute the *pāyasam* among his three queens. By the grace of the Lord, his queens gave birth to four princes who were named *Rāma*, *Lakṣmaṇa*, *Bharata* and *Śatrughna*. *Rāma* and *Bharata* were born to queens *Kausalyā* and *Kaikeyī* respectively, while *Lakṣmaṇa* and *Śatrughna* were born to queen *Sumitrā*. *Rāma's* stature, gentleness coupled with courage and wisdom made him a young hero, loved by all in the kingdom. Even King *Daśaratha* was more fond of *Rāma* than his other sons, as *Rāma* was devoted to him and cared for him deeply.

One day, Sage *Viśvāmitra* came to *Daśaratha's* palace and asked the king to send *Rāma* with him to the forest. He needed *Rāma's* help in killing the demons that were interfering with the fire ritual being performed by the sage.

King *Daśaratha* being offered *Pāyasa*

Rāmāvatāra contd...

At first, *Daśaratha* was reluctant to send *Rāma* as he loved him very much and feared for his life. Sage *Vasiṣṭha*, confident of *Rāma's* skills and prowess, reassured him and the king sent *Rāma* with the sage alongwith *Lakṣmaṇa*. During their journey, the princes learnt archery and other disciplines of knowledge from the sage. Upon reaching *Siddhāśrama*, the sage's hermitage, *Rāma* and *Lakṣmaṇa* protected the sacrifice by killing the demons and carried the ritual through its completion.

Pleased with the accomplishments of the young princes, *Viśvāmitra* took them to the assembly of King *Janaka* of *Mithilā*. He wanted the princes to see the bow of Lord *Śiva* which many great heroes had failed to even lift. King *Janaka* had offered his beautiful daughter, Princess *Sītā*, in marriage to anyone who would break the bow. *Rāma* effortlessly lifted the bow, strung it, and drawing the bow, broke it instantly. *Rāma*, thus, won *Sītā* in marriage. His brothers also married the princesses from *Janaka's* family. The princes along with their brides and *Daśaratha* returned to *Ayodhyā* and lived happily for a number of years.

As *Daśaratha* was becoming old, one day he decided to coronate *Rāma* as the *yuvarājā*, crown prince, with the consent of the elders. Everyone was happy to hear about it and began preparing for the coronation, which was to take place the following day. In the meanwhile, *Mantarā*, a servant-maid of *Kaikeyī*, planted the seeds of jealousy in *Kaikeyī's* mind against *Kausalyā*, the senior queen. She suggested to *Kaikeyī* to encash her two boons which *Daśaratha* had once given her, by asking for *Rāma* to be sent to the forest for fourteen years and for coronating *Bharata* to the throne of *Ayodhyā*. *Kaikeyī*, influenced by *Mantarā*, did as she was told.

I. Jigsaw Puzzle

Colour the areas marked as per the colour-key given below. Now see what *Tāṭakā* changed herself into?

Colour-key: Dots - grey, V - violet, G - green, W - white, and the rest as per your imagination.

Rāmāvatāra contd...

Daśaratha was shocked at *Kaikeyī's* claim of the two boons, but bound as he was by his promise, he could not refuse *Kaikeyī*. *Rāma* honoured his father's words and left for the forest. As a true *pativratā*, a devoted wife, *Sītā* also accompanied *Rāma*. *Rāma* could not dissuade the persistent *Lakṣmaṇa* who also decided to accompany them. Soon after, another tragedy struck the royal family when *Daśaratha* passed away in grief of separation from his beloved son.

Bharata who was in his maternal uncle's place all this time, was sent for by Sage *Vasiṣṭha*. Upon arriving in *Ayodhyā*, *Bharata* came to know of his mother's cruel deeds and his father's death which had been due to the grief of separation from *Rāma*. He condemned her for her actions and disowned her as his mother. Performing his father's last rites, he decided to bring *Rāma* back to *Ayodhyā* and set out for *Citrakūṭa* where *Rāma* was staying.

Bharata met *Rāma* and pleaded with him to return, but *Rāma* stood firm on his commitment to keep his father's promise to *Kaikeyī*. Instead, he asked the reluctant *Bharata* to return to *Ayodhyā* and rule the kingdom. *Bharata* finally agreed to rule as a proxy for the fourteen year period of exile and installed *Rāma's* sandals on the throne as a symbol of his rule.

In the forest, *Rāma* visited many hermitages and earned the grace of the sages. He killed a number of *rākṣasas* who harassed the sages in their life of asceticism, and thus gave them his protection.

II. Find the qualities of *Rāma* (listed in Column A) in the word game. Look up, down and across.

H	E	L	P	F	U	L	C
U	F	O	E	R	C	O	L
M	A	V	A	I	H	G	E
B	B	I	C	E	E	E	A
L	R	N	E	N	E	N	N
E	I	G	F	D	R	T	D
I	F	H	U	L	F	L	A
O	M	L	L	Y	U	E	A
K	I	N	D	E	L	M	H
T	R	U	T	H	F	U	L
E	S	I	W	R	R	I	D
D	H	A	R	M	I	C	H

Rāmāvatāra contd...

While they were staying in *Pañcavaṭī* on the banks of River *Godāvarī*, one day, a *rākṣasī Śūrpaṇakhā*, arrived at the *āśrama*. She fell in love with *Rāma* and asked him to marry her. *Rāma* in humorous jest told her to go to *Lakṣmaṇa*. *Lakṣmaṇa*, too, joined his brother in the humour and directed her back to *Rāma* telling her that she would be a mere servant if she married him, since he was only *Rāma's* servant and that *Rāma* would like her better than *Sītā* who lacked beauty. Thus being sent back and forth, *Śūrpaṇakhā* lost her patience and seeing *Sītā* as the stumbling block in her marrying *Rāma*, she furiously advanced towards her. *Lakṣmaṇa* promptly took his sword and chopped off her nose and ears.

Angered by the humiliation, *Śūrpaṇakhā* went to her brother *Rāvaṇa* and pleaded with him to take revenge on the two brothers. She evoked in him a passion for *Sītā* by describing her beauty to him and asked him to capture *Sītā* and make her his wife. *Rāvaṇa* sought *Mārīca's* help, compelling him to take the form of a beautiful golden deer and attract *Sītā's* attention in *Pañcavaṭī*. Transforming himself into a captivating golden deer, *Mārīca* wandered around the *āśrama* playfully. Enchanted by the charming beauty of the animal, *Sītā* called out to *Rāma* and *Lakṣmaṇa* and asked them to capture the deer and bring it to her. Unable to resist her entreaties, *Rāma* went behind the deer, asking *Lakṣmaṇa* to look after *Sītā*. After a long chase, *Rāma* sent an arrow at his target. As the arrow pierced the animal, simulating the voice of *Rāma*, it cried out for help and fell dead.

Sītā heard the cries and fearing for *Rāma's* life, she appealed to *Lakṣmaṇa* to go and help *Rāma*. *Lakṣmaṇa* sensed danger for *Sītā* and refused to leave her alone. *Sītā's* fears turned into anger against *Lakṣmaṇa*. She assailed him of bad character and ascribed ulterior motives of his desire to marry her. *Lakṣmaṇa* reluctantly left her. Seeing *Sītā* alone, *Rāvaṇa* approached her in the guise of a monk and kidnapped her. Overpowering *Jaṭāyu*, an eagle bird, who resisted him on his flight, *Rāvaṇa* reached *Laṅkā* and kept *Sītā* in the *Aśokavana*, the royal grove, closely guarded by a number of *rākṣasīs*.

Rāvaṇa **kidnaps** ***Sītā***

Rāmāvatāra contd...

After killing *Mārīca*, *Rāma* hurried towards the *āśrama* where on the way he met *Lakṣmaṇa* running towards him. As they reached the *āśrama*, they saw the *āśrama* empty, confirming their fears. *Rāma* wept bitterly and ran all over searching for *Sītā*. *Lakṣmaṇa* tried to console him and calm him down.

After a long search in the forest, they came across the *vānara* chief *Sugrīva*, who was living in exile in the *Ṛṣyamūka* hill. *Sugrīva's* elder brother, *Vāli* had usurped his wife *Rumā* besides exiling him. *Rāma* and *Sugrīva* struck a bond of friendship. *Rāma* promised *Sugrīva* that he would help him to get rid of *Vāli* and gain back his wife and the kingdom of *Kiṣkindhā*. *Sugrīva*, in turn, promised all assistance to *Rāma* in his efforts to find *Sītā*.

Confident of *Rāma's* prowess and valour, *Sugrīva* challenged *Vāli* to a fight. In the encounter that took place between the two brothers, *Rāma* sent an arrow at *Vāli* and killed him. Arranging to perform the obsequies of *Vāli*, *Rāma* coronated *Sugrīva* as the king of *Kiṣkindhā*. *Aṅgada*, son of *Vāli*, was appointed the crown prince.

Sugrīva, on his part, sent his *vānaras* in all the four directions to search for *Sītā*. *Hanumān*, the most powerful and wise minister of *Sugrīva*, went towards the south. Guided by *Sampāti*, brother of *Jaṭāyu*, *Hanumān* crossed the ocean and reached *Laṅkā*. After a long search, *Hanumān* discovered *Sītā* in the *Aśokavana*. Giving her the signet ring of *Rāma*, *Hanumān* assured her that *Rāma* would soon return with the *vānara* army and destroying *Rāvaṇa* in a battle, would relieve her of her sufferings.

III. Mark it with an X.

Mark the "odd one out" (the one that does not belong in the group).

Group 1

____ *Rāma* ____ *Sītā* ____ *Daśaratha*

____ *Janaka* ____ *Maṇḍodarī*

Group 2

____ *Rāvaṇa* ____ *Sugrīva* ____ *Kumbhakarṇa*

____ *Vibhīṣaṇa* ____ *Śurpaṇakhā*

Group 3

____ *Sugrīva* ____ *Aṅgada* ____ *Guha*

____ *Hanumān* ____ *Vāli*

Group 4

____ *Lakṣmaṇa* ____ *Bharata* ____ *Śatrughna*

____ *Kaikeyī* ____ *Rāma*

Group 5

____ *Mantharā* ____ *Daśaratha* ____ *Sumitrā*

____ *Kaikeyī* ____ *Kausalyā*

Rāmāvatāra contd...

After taking leave of *Sītā*, *Hanumān* was ready for his return journey when he thought of doing something that would give him a first hand information about *Rāvaṇa's* army strength as well as instill confidence in *Sītā* regarding the strength of the *vānara* army of *Rāma*. He instigated a fight with the *rākṣasas* by destroying the beautiful royal grove, *Aśokavana*. Killing many *rākṣasas* in the fight that ensued, he encountered *Rāvaṇa's* son, *Indrajit* and was bound by *Indrajit's Brahmāstra*. When the *rākṣasas* tied him with other materials, the divine *astra* lost its power and *Hanumān* became free. However, welcoming the opportunity to have an audience with *Rāvaṇa*, *Hanumān* allowed himself to be dragged to *Rāvaṇa's* court.

Hanumān boldly asked *Rāvaṇa* to return *Sītā* and ask for *Rāma's* forgiveness or face the dire consequences in the battlefield. Angered by *Hanumān's* bold statements, *Rāvaṇa* punished him by setting his tail on fire. Hearing about the punishment, *Sītā* prayed to Lord *Agni* with whose grace, *Hanumān* remained unaffected by the heat and flames. *Hanumān* burnt the entire city of *Laṅkā* with the fire on his tail. Having accomplished his selfappointed task, *Hanumān* then put out the fire by dipping his tail in the sea and returning to *Rāma*, reported the happy news of *Sītā's* discovery.

Rāma was now anxious to cross the ocean with a huge army and reach *Laṅkā*. *Sugrīva* encouraged him with words of support and they marched towards the ocean. Soon they reached the foot of Mount *Mahendra* and *Rāma* ascended the peak and surveyed the vast expanse of the sea.

IV. Delete

Cut out the wrong answers:

1. After taking leave of *Sītā*, *Hanumān* wanted to
   a) run away
   b) meet *Rāvaṇa*
   c) stay at *Aśokavana*

2. *Hanumān* wanted to teach *Rāvaṇa*
   a) how to sing
   b) how to leap in the air
   c) a lesson

3. When *Hanumān* destroyed *Aśokavana*, *Rāvaṇa* was
   a) jumping with joy
   b) very angry
   c) shedding tears

4. *Indrajit* tied up *Hanumān* with
   a) thorny creepers
   b) big iron chain
   c) the *Brahmāstra*

5. The *rākṣasas* dragged *Hanumān* to
   a) the beach
   b) *Rāvaṇa's* court
   c) a swimming pool

V. What do I say?

Write in your own words a dialogue between *Hanumān*, and *Rāma* in the speech bubbles provided.

I found Mother *Sītā*, My Lord!

....

....
....
....
....
....
.....

O *Hanumān*! How happy am I to...................

....

....

....

....

....

Rāmāvatāra contd...

At *Laṅkā*, *Rāvaṇa*, shaken by the havoc caused by a mere monkey, called his council of ministers to discuss the future course of action. While every one in the court spoke in support of *Rāvaṇa*, *Vibhīṣaṇa*, the virtuous brother of *Rāvaṇa*, argued for *Sītā's* return. Annoyed with *Vibhīṣaṇa*, *Rāvaṇa* hurled harsh words at him. Seeing that he no longer had a role in *Laṅkā*, *Vibhīṣaṇa* crossed the sea and sought refuge in *Rāma*. In keeping with his principle of accepting anyone who came to him, *Rāma* embraced *Vibhīṣaṇa* lovingly.

Soon a bridge was built across the ocean with the help of the *vānaras* and the entire army crossed over to *Laṅkā*. *Rāma* sent *Aṅgada* on a peace mission to *Rāvaṇa*. But *Rāvaṇa*, refused to return *Sītā* and the war was declared.

In the fight, many great warriors of *Rāvaṇa's* army such as *Jambumālī*, *Prahasta*, *Atikāya*, *Triśiras*, *Kumbha* and *Nikumbha* were killed by the *vānara* chiefs. *Kumbhakarṇa*, *Rāvaṇa's* brother was killed by *Rāma*, while *Lakṣmaṇa* with the help of *Vibhīṣaṇa*, killed *Indrajit*. Finally, a great battle ensued between *Rāma* and *Rāvaṇa*. Both sent powerful *astras* at each other and one was countered by the other with more powerful weapons. Many celestial beings witnessed the battle from the sky. At the end, *Rāma* invoked Lord *Brahmā* and sent his *Brahmāstra* piercing *Rāvaṇa's* chest and *Rāvaṇa* fell dead. There was rejoice in all the three worlds. *Rāma* crowned *Vibhīṣaṇa* as the king of *Laṅkā*. Establishing *Sītā's* purity through a fire test, *Rāma* reunited with *Sītā*, and returned to *Ayodhyā*.

Bharata was rejoiced to see *Rāma* back at *Ayodhyā* on the completion of the fourteenth year. He asked *Rāma* to wear his sandals again and *Rāma* was coronated the king of *Ayodhyā* with *Bharata* as crown prince.

Rāma ruled *Ayodhyā* for many years. There was justice everywhere and people had no fear of *adharma*. It was an ideal kingdom ruled by an ideal king, Lord *Rāma*. Having achieved the purpose of his incarnation, Lord *Rāma* returned to his abode at the end of his rule.

KṚṢṆĀVATĀRA

Lord *Kṛṣṇa* was born in the lunar dynasty in which *Yadu*, the son of *Yayāti*, was a great king. *Kṛṣṇa* was called *Yadukula Tilaka*, as he was the foremost among the *Yādavas*, the descendants of *Yadu*.

Śūra was one of the chief rulers of the *Yādavas*. He ruled the kingdom of *Mathurā* and *Śūrasena*. He had a son named *Vasudeva* who married *Devakī*, the daughter of *Devaka*, *Ugrasena's* brother.

After the wedding, *Vasudeva* was returning to his palace with *Devakī*, in a chariot driven by *Kaṃsa*, *Ugrasena's* son. At that time, a voice from the heaven addressed *Kaṃsa* and declared that the eighth child of *Devakī* would be the cause of his death. Fear gripped him and in an anxiety to protect himself, *Kaṃsa* stopped the chariot and seizing *Devakī* by her hair, raised his sword to kill her. *Vasudeva*, pleaded for her life reminding him that *Devakī* was indeed his sister and a newly wedded bride. When *Kaṃsa* still saw no good reason to spare her, *Vasudeva* offered to hand over the babies to him as soon as they were born. *Kaṃsa* had trust in *Vasudeva's* words and spared *Devakī's* life.

In due course of time, the first baby was born and *Vasudeva* offered the child to *Kaṃsa*. *Kaṃsa*, pleased with *Vasudeva's* honesty, returned the child as only the eighth one was to be his enemy. In the meanwhile, Sage *Nārada*, who always had a noble purpose behind his seemingly unpleasant acts, went to *Kaṃsa* and warned him that the cowherds of *Gokula* and the relatives of *Vasudeva* were all manifestations of the Lord and thus instilled fear in him from all the children of *Devakī*. *Kaṃsa* immediately imprisoned *Vasudeva* and *Devakī*, and killed all their sons as and when they were born. He also put his own father *Ugrasena* in jail and proclaiming himself the ruler of *Mathurā*, went about destroying the *Yādavas*.

I. Fill in these speech bubbles.

O! *Kaṃsa* ______________

I will ______________ ______________ ______________

Please do not ______________

Voice from the

Kamsa

Vasudeva

Devakī is ______________ ______________ ______________

Ugrasena

O king! ______________ ______________ ______________ ______________

I beg you ______________ __- ______________

Guards

Devakī

Kṛṣṇāvatāra contd...

When the seventh child was to be born to *Devakī*, the Lord with his *yogamāyā*, creative power, transferred the embryo from *Devakī* to *Rohiṇī*, another wife of *Vasudeva* who was living in *Gokula*. The child born to *Rohiṇī* was named *Balarāma*. The guards in the prison reported to *Kaṃsa* the abortion of the seventh child. When *Devakī* conceived the eighth child, her form shone with all lustre. *Kaṃsa* knew that the Lord had entered *Devakī's* womb. He was prompted to kill her at once. But the fear of incurring the sin of killing a pregnant woman restrained him and *Kaṃsa* waited for the Lord to be born.

That night there was thunder, lightning and a heavy down pour of rains. At midnight, *Kṛṣṇa* was born in the dark cell. The Lord instructed *Vasudeva* that he should be taken to *Nandagopa's* house in *Gokula*. *Vasudeva's* shackles automatically got loosened.

Placing baby *Kṛṣṇa* in a basket, *Vasudeva* proceeded to go to *Gokula*. As he carried the baby and left the prison cell, the gates opened and the guards fell asleep. The serpent king, *Ādiśeṣa*, held his hooded head as an umbrella protecting the Lord from the wind and rains. The *Yamunā*, which was in spate, offered a passage for *Vasudeva* to cross over. *Vasudeva* reached the house of *Nandagopa* in *Gokula* and placing his son by the side of the sleeping *Yaśodā*, wife of *Nandagopa*, carried her newly born baby back to the prison cell in *Mathurā*. As *Vasudeva* crossed each gate, the gates closed automatically and he was in shackles as before.

II. Match the magical events.

1) The guards a) suddenly opened

2) The chains on *Vasudeva*'s hands and feet b) parted to make a path

3) The prison doors c) slept soundly

4) The serpent *Ādiśeṣa* d) became unconscious

5) The river waters e) held its hood up

6) Every one at *Gokula* f) fell off

Vasudeva carrying *Kṛṣṇa* to Gokula

Kṛṣṇāvatāra contd...

As soon as *Kaṃsa* came to know that the eighth child was born to *Devakī*, he rushed to the prison cell. Despite *Devakī's* fervent prayers to spare the life of her daughter, *Kaṃsa* picked the child to kill her when the baby flew off his hand taking the form of Goddess *Durgā* and warned him that his enemy had already taken birth and killing *Devakī's* children any more would only be in vain. Saying this, she vanished.

The miracle of the baby flying off his hand and the words of the Goddess created a deep impact on *Kaṃsa* and his attitude towards *Devakī* and *Vasudeva* changed. He released them and sought forgiveness for his wrong actions. But upon reaching the palace, *Kaṃsa* was counselled by his ministers to destroy all the children less than one year old and *Kaṃsa* promptly ordered for the killing of the babies.

In *Gokula*, *Yaśodā* did not know whether she had conceived a male or a female baby as they had all been overpowered by sleep soon after the baby's birth. After *Vasudeva* left, they woke up and discovered that a son had been born to *Yaśodā*. *Nanda* performed the *jātakarma*, the birth ceremony and gave away a lot of wealth in charity. The entire village celebrated the birth of *Kṛṣṇa*.

On the advice of *Kaṃsa*, the demoness *Pūtanā* was sent to the village of the cowherds to kill all the infants less than one year old. *Pūtanā* came to *Gokula* and won the hearts of the *gopīs* by the beautiful form she had assumed. She entered *Nandagopa's* house and saw the baby in the cradle. Seeing no one around, she took the baby on her lap and suckled him with her breasts that were smeared with poison. The Lord sucked her life through the breast and assuming her original form, *Pūtanā* fell dead.

Kṛṣṇāvatāra contd...

Rohiṇī and *Yaśodā* saw the frightening scene of the huge monstress lying dead and *Kṛṣṇa* playing on her bosom. They purified the baby with rituals and prayers to ward off any evil effect of the demoness on the baby and thanked the Lord for saving the baby's life.

Once when *Kṛṣṇa* was about one year old, a demon named *Tṛṇāvarta* came in the form of a dust storm and carried *Kṛṣṇa* away to the sky. The demon had been sent by *Kaṃsa*. Suddenly, *Tṛṇāvarta* felt that he could not carry *Kṛṣṇa* any further as *Kṛṣṇa's* weight had tremendously increased. He assumed his original form when *Kṛṣṇa* catching hold of his throat, killed him. The demon fell dead and the storm abated. No one could understand what happened in the fury of the storm. But everyone was overjoyed to find *Kṛṣṇa* amidst them again and they did not care any more about how the *asura* got killed.

Kṛṣṇa and *Balarāma* delighted everyone in *Gokula* through their games and pranks. *Kṛṣṇa* would tease the *gopīs* by stealing the curds and butter from their homes. *Yaśodā* could never scold *Kṛṣṇa* as he would always plead ignorance. Captivated by a mere smile of the mischievous *Kṛṣṇa*, the *gopīs* too would forget their anger.

One day *Kṛṣṇa* was playing with other children when *Balarāma* came running to *Yaśodā* and told her that *Kṛṣṇa* had put a handful of mud into his mouth. *Yaśodā* rushed to her child's rescue, but *Kṛṣṇa* denied that he had eaten any mud, and accused others of telling a lie. *Yaśodā* asked him to open his mouth and when he did, she saw the entire universe in him. She also saw in him *Gokula* as well as herself looking into *Kṛṣṇa's* mouth. She realised that *Kṛṣṇa* was not just a child but the Lord himself. She could not believe her eyes and wondered whether the experience was a dream or real. *Kṛṣṇa* quickly closed his mouth and *Yaśodā*, forgetting the incident, began to treat *Kṛṣṇa* as her son.

III. Help Me

Help ***Kṛṣṇa*** climb the rope to reach the pot of butter.

Kṛṣṇāvatāra contd...

Tired of *Kṛṣṇa's* pranks, *Yaśodā* one day tied *Kṛṣṇa* to a wooden mortar with a string and went to complete her household chores. *Kṛṣṇa* drawing the mortar behind him, went towards the courtyard and crawled between two tall trees standing side by side. As he pulled the mortar further, the trees fell with a loud crash. *Kṛṣṇa* thereby released the two *yakṣas*, celestials, who in their previous birth had been cursed to become those tall trees. Upon hearing the noise *Yaśodā* rushed to the site and was relieved that *Kṛṣṇa* had escaped unhurt. She regretted having tied him, and instantly let him free.

As a child, *Kṛṣṇa* playfully killed many more *asuras*, sent by *Kaṃsa*, such as *Vatsāsura*, who came in the guise of a calf, *Bakāsura*, who came in the form of heron, and *Aghāsura*, who lay on the path of *Kṛṣṇa* and his playmates in the form of a huge python with his mouth open.

As the two brothers grew older, they were assigned the task of tending the cows. They took the cows out daily for grazing in *Vṛndāvana*. One day, *Śrīdāma*, a playmate, informed *Kṛṣṇa* of a palmyra grove nearby which was laden with fruits. He requested *Kṛṣṇa* to get some fruits for them, but warned him about *Dhenukāsura* who had been haunting the grove in the guise of a donkey. *Kṛṣṇa* and *Balarāma* entered the grove and started shaking the trees for the fruits. *Dhenukāsura* heard the noise and rushed towards them. *Balarāma*, seizing the donkey by its front legs whirled it and dashed it against the trees. *Dhenukāsura* thus fell dead and the grove was released from the *asura's* hold.

IV. Find and colour *Kṛṣṇa* as he plays with his friends.

Kṛṣṇāvatāra contd...

Kṛṣṇa with his playmates and the cows then reached the banks of *Yamunā*, also known as *Kālindi*. Feeling thirsty, the cows and cowherds drank the waters of a lake on the bed of *Yamunā* when they instantly fell dead. *Kṛṣṇa* revived them and ascertaining the cause, found out that the waters had become poisonous due to the black serpent *Kāliya* who had inhabited the lake.

He jumped into the lake from the top of a *kadamba* tree on the bank. *Kāliya* surfaced and catching hold of *Kṛṣṇa*, coiled around him. *Nanda*, *Yaśodā* with *Rohiṇī* and other cowherds, rushed to the bank of *Yamunā* in search of *Kṛṣṇa*. Seeing *Kṛṣṇa* in the serpent's grip they were frightened and prayed for his safety. *Kṛṣṇa* expanded his body and released himself from *Kāliya's* hold. After tiring *Kāliya* with his tricks, he leapt on the broad hoods of the serpent and danced. *Kāliya's* wives prayed for the serpent's life. *Kṛṣṇa* spared *Kāliya*, but told him to live in the isolated island of *Ramaṇaka* in the ocean. *Kṛṣṇa* then came out of the lake and everyone felt relieved to see him unscathed. Embracing him with joy, they all returned to *Vṛndāvana*.

Once the cowherds were preparing for their annual worship of *Indra*, the deity of rains, when *Kṛṣṇa* asked them to divert all oblations meant for *Indra* to the worship of *Govardhana* mountain, the brahmins and the cows. Proud of his position, *Indra* felt insulted by this gesture of *Kṛṣṇa*. He commanded the *samvartaka* clouds to bring about torrential rains in *Vṛndāvana*. *Kṛṣṇa*, who was then tending the cows with his playmates, lifted the *Govardhana* mountain and held it on his hand for seven days and protected all of them. Amazed at *Kṛṣṇa's* feat, and ashamed of himself, *Indra* stopped the rains. Falling at *Kṛṣṇa's* feet he sought his forgiveness and praised him as *Govinda*, the protector of the universe.

V. Spot the differences.

Spot at least six differences in these two pictures and circle them with different colours.

Kṛṣṇāvatāra contd...

The *gopīs* had been anxiously awaiting the arrival of autumn, when *Kṛṣṇa* had promised to play *rāsakrīḍā* with them. The autumn finally set in. On a moonlit night, *Kṛṣṇa* went to the banks of *Yamunā* in *Vṛndāvana*, and started playing his flute. All the *gopīs* rushed to him leaving their household chores unfinished and even unmindful of their appearance. *Kṛṣṇa* appeared as many and danced and played with every *gopī*. Whenever the *gopīs* became conscious of themselves and their beauty, *Kṛṣṇa* would disappear. Grieving over the pangs of separation, they would long for him and pray that he might appear again. *Kṛṣṇa* would then appear before them and comfort them with his love. The long night thus came to an end and *Kṛṣṇa* sent the unwilling *gopīs* back to their homes.

In *Mathurā*, Sage *Nārada* once visited *Kaṃsa* and revealed to him the secrets of *Kṛṣṇa's* birth. He informed him that *Kṛṣṇa* was the eighth son of *Devakī*, who was being raised by *Nanda* and *Yaśodā*. Infuriated upon knowing this, he again put *Devakī* and *Vasudeva* in chains. He sent in vain *Keśī*, a demon, to slay *Kṛṣṇa*.

Kaṃsa then summoned his ministers, wrestlers and elephant-keepers, and planned another strategy. He decided to perform a *dhanur-yāga* and organised a wrestling tournament in public as part of the celebrations. He planned to invite *Kṛṣṇa* and *Balarāma* and told the chief elephant-keeper to have *Kuvalayapīḍa*, the mighty elephant, crush the brothers to death when they entered the wrestling grounds. If this failed, he arranged for *Cāṇūra* and *Muṣṭika* to kill them in a wrestling game.

Kaṃsa then called *Akrūra*, a relative of *Vasudeva*, to go to *Nanda's* place and invite *Kṛṣṇa* and *Balarāma* to *Mathurā* for the *dhanur-yāga*. *Akrūra* was pleased to meet *Kṛṣṇa* and invited him to *Mathurā* for the function. The *gopīs* and cowherds could not bear the separation from *Kṛṣṇa*. Leaving every one grieving, *Kṛṣṇa* mounted the chariot with his brother and left for *Mathurā*.

VI. Write out an invitation from King *Kaṃsa* to *Nandagopa*.

Dear Chief

____________________,

I am glad to

____

for a ____________________________

We will also have

Do come with your sons

______________ and

The matches will be held at

____

(Sign) __________________

(Place) _________________

Kṛṣṇāvatāra contd...

Upon reaching *Mathurā*, the brothers alighted from the chariot and walked in the streets. Forcing their way into the sacrificial hall of *Kaṃsa*, *Kṛṣṇa* effortlessly broke the huge bow kept for worship. At the entrance to the wrestling grounds, *Kṛṣṇa* saw *Kuvalayapīḍa*. Catching hold of the elephant by its trunk, he hurled it on the ground. *Cāṇūra* and *Muṣṭika* met their ends in the hands of *Kṛṣṇa* and *Balarāma* respectively in a wrestling game. Seeing his renowned wrestlers fall, *Kaṃsa* insulted *Kṛṣṇa*. *Kṛṣṇa* got annoyed and dragging *Kaṃsa* down from the throne threw him hard on the ground. Dropping his body weight on *Kaṃsa*, *Kṛṣṇa* crushed him to death.

Kṛṣṇa then hurried to his parents *Devakī* and *Vasudeva*, and freed them. He also released *Ugrasena* from the prison and made him the king of *Mathurā*.

With the help of Sage *Garga*, *Vasudeva* then performed the *upanayana-saṃskāra* for *Kṛṣṇa* and *Balarāma*. The brothers went to the *gurukula* and studied at the feet of *Guru Sāndīpani* at Ujjain. After completion of their studies, they returned to *Mathurā* and spent a lot of time with *Devakī* and *Vasudeva* listening to all the happenings in their families during the time they were growing up in *Gokula*. *Vasudeva* narrated the story of his sister *Kuntī* as follows:

Kuntī had married *Pāṇḍu* and had five children called *Pāṇḍavas*. *Pāṇḍu's* brother *Dhṛtarāṣṭra* had one hundred sons of whom *Duryodhana* was the eldest. After *Pāṇḍu's* death in the forest, *Kuntī* had returned to *Hastināpura* with her five sons. As the princes were young, *Dhṛtarāṣṭra* had become the ruler of *Hastināpura*. *Duryodhana*, due to his jealousy towards the *Pāṇḍavas*, was ill-treating them.

VII. Complete the answer.

Complete these answers by choosing the right options from below:

1. Why was *Kaṃsa* worried?

   Kaṃsa was worried ______________________________

2. What did *Muṣṭika* call *Kṛṣṇa* for?

   Muṣṭika called *Kṛṣṇa* for __________________________

3. What did *Kṛṣṇa* do after pulling *Kaṃsa* down by his hair?

   After pulling *Kaṃsa* down by his hair _________________

4. Why were the people of *Mathurā* happy to see *Kaṃsa* dead?

   The people were happy to see *Kaṃsa* dead ______________

5. Why did *Kṛṣṇa* rush to prison?

   Kṛṣṇa rushed to the prison _________________________

i) to free *Devakī* and *Vasudeva*.

ii) because *Kṛṣṇa* had broken the mighty bow.

iii) because he was a cruel King.

iv) a wrestling match.

v) *Kṛṣṇa* killed *Kaṃsa*.

Kṛṣṇa Kills *Kaṃsa*

Kṛṣṇāvatāra contd...

Thus recounting the story, *Vasudeva* asked *Kṛṣṇa* to help *Kuntī*, his aunt, and bring joy in her life. *Kṛṣṇa* sent *Akrūra* to *Hastināpura* to get information regarding the goings on there. He also sent a message to *Nanda* and others through *Uddhava*, to relieve them of their agony of separation from him.

In the meanwhile, *Jarāsandha*, *Kaṃsa's* father-in-law, had begun to repeatedly attack *Mathurā*. *Kṛṣṇa* asked *Viśvakarmā* to construct a new city called *Dvārakā*. He shifted every one to *Dvārakā* and becoming the ruler of *Dvārakā*, protected the lives of the people.

While in *Dvārakā*, he received a message from *Rukmiṇī*, daughter of *Bhīṣmaka*, the king of *Vidarbha*, asking *Kṛṣṇa* to marry her. She conveyed to *Kṛṣṇa* that her brother *Rukmi* had arranged her marriage with *Śiśupāla*, the king of *Cedi* much against her wishes and prayed that *Kṛṣṇa* come and take her away. *Kṛṣṇa* took away *Rukmiṇī* from the temple of Goddess *Pārvatī* on the morning of the marriage when she went there for worship and then married her. A son was born to them and was named *Pradyumna*. When *Pradyumna* came of age, he married *Rukmāvatī*, the daughter of *Rukmi*, and they had a son named *Aniruddha*.

Once *Kṛṣṇa* was falsely accused of stealing the *Śymantaka* gem, the gem of prosperity. The jewel was owned by *Satrājit* of the *Yādava* clan. With great effort, *Kṛṣṇa* retrieved the jewel and restored it to *Satrājit*, who in turn gave his daughter *Satyabhāmā* in marriage to *Kṛṣṇa*.

After *Arjuna* had won *Draupadī* in a *svayaṃvara*, the *Paṇḍavas* were in the forest living in a potter's house. During that time, *Kṛṣṇa* went and met his cousins for the first time. A friendship grew between *Kṛṣṇa* and *Arjuna*. *Kṛṣṇa* promised to be with the five brothers through all their troubles. He then returned to *Dvārakā*. At that time, *Indra* asked *Kṛṣṇa's* help in killing the demon *Narakāsura*, the son of Mother Earth. *Narakāsura* lived in a city called *Prāgjyotiṣa*. *Kṛṣṇa* killed him in a fight with his *Sudarśana* disc. *Kṛṣṇa* also chastened *Bāṇāsura*, the son of *Bali* and *Bāṇāsura* gave his daughter *Uṣā* in marriage to *Aniruddha*.

Yudhiṣṭhira the eldest of the *Pāṇḍavas* and the king of *Indraprastha*, once arranged to perform a *Rājasūya* sacrifice. *Kṛṣṇa* went to *Indraprastha* to participate in the sacrifice. The *Rājasūya* could only be performed when one had conquered all the kings. *Jarāsandha*, the king of *Magadha*, was the only one who refused to surrender. *Bhīma*, *Arjuna* and *Kṛṣṇa* went to *Magadha* to fight *Jarāsandha* and defeat him. *Bhīma* and *Jarāsandha* fought a long battle of wrestling. Finally, with *Kṛṣṇa's* guidance, *Bhīma* felled *Jarāsandha* to the ground and killed him.

Kṛṣṇāvatāra contd...

Yudhiṣṭhira invited all the kings for the *Rājasūya-yāga*. In the assembly, he gave the place of honour to *Kṛṣṇa* and worshipped him as stipulated for the function. *Śiśupāla* did not approve of this gesture and verbally abused *Kṛṣṇa* for a long time. When *Śiśupāla* did not relent, *Kṛṣṇa* used his disc and severed his head. Thus getting rid of unwanted and destructive forces, the *yāga* was performed and completed in a grand manner.

After spending some time with his cousins in *Indraprastha*, *Kṛṣṇa* returned to *Dvārakā*. One day *Sudāmā*, *Kṛṣṇa's gurukula* friend prompted by his wife, came to *Kṛṣṇa* to seek his help in being relieved of his poverty. Joyous upon seeing his friend after many years, *Kṛṣṇa* greeted him with a warm embrace. He recounted the experiences of their *gurukula* days, and revived their bond of friendship. *Sudāmā* had brought for *Kṛṣṇa* a handful of flattened rice which *Kṛṣṇa* readily ate with pleasure. *Kṛṣṇa* extended all hospitality to *Sudāmā* for his stay. Overwhelmed with *Kṛṣṇa's* love and affection, *Sudāmā* returned home without asking for any help. Upon reaching his place, he saw a mansion in the place of his thatched house. His wife dressed in silk garments and adorned with gold ornaments looked very beautiful. *Sudāmā* felt grateful for the blessing showered upon them and enjoyed the wealth and prosperity with humility and devotion.

VIII. Matching

Identify the relationships by drawing lines to connect the words.

	WHO?	RELATED TO WHOM?	HOW?
1.	*Vasudeva*	*Kṛṣṇa*	Brother
2.	*Kṛṣṇa*	*Kaṃsa*	Friend
3.	*Balarāma*	*Nanda*	Sister
4.	*Devakī*	*Sudāmā*	First cousin
5.	*Yaśodā*	*Arjuna*	Wife
6.	*Kṛṣṇa*	*Vasudeva*	Sister
7.	*Kuntī*	*Kṛṣṇa*	Father

Kṛṣṇāvatāra contd...

In *Hastināpura*, the *Pāṇḍavas* having lost everything in a game of dice with *Duryodhana* were exiled to the forest for thirteen years. After the thirteen long years of exile was over, the *Pāṇḍavas* returned and asked for their share of kingdom. *Duryodhana* refused to return the kingdom. *Kṛṣṇa* went on a peace mission to *Hastināpura* but failed and the two armies assembled at *Kurukṣetra*. *Kṛṣṇa* was driving *Arjuna's* chariot. When the war was about to begin, to the surprise and dismay of all, *Arjuna* refused to fight. He felt confused about his *dharma* towards his teachers and relatives for whom he had love and regard. With dispassion in his heart for the kingdom, he surrendered to *Kṛṣṇa* and asked him to teach him that knowledge which would give him the ultimate goal of life. *Kṛṣṇa* gave him the teachings of *sāṅkhya*, self-knowledge and *yoga*, the means that would help *Arjuna* acquire the proper disposition of mind for gaining the knowledge. These words of *Kṛṣṇa* are known as the *Bhagavad Gītā*. Cleared of his doubts and vagueness, *Arjuna* fought the war and the *Pāṇḍavas* won.

With the *Mahābhārata* war, *Kṛṣṇa's* mission on earth ended. He returned to *Dvārakā* and prepared for his final departure. *Balarāma*, too, returned to *Dvārakā* after his pilgrimage which he had undertaken during the war. He decided to give up his life through *yoga*. *Kṛṣṇa* went to *Prabhāsa-tīrtha* with the *Yādavas*. In *Prabhāsa*, the *Yādavas*, intoxicated with drinks, fought among themselves and killed each other, wiping out the entire clan of *Yādavas*. Witnessing the scene of destruction, *Kṛṣṇa* walked out, and proceeding alone in the forest, sat under an *aśvattha* tree. A hunter, seeing *Kṛṣṇa's* yellow silken cloth and mistaking him for a deer, sent an arrow and fatally hurt *Kṛṣṇa* on his feet. *Kṛṣṇa* left the mortal world and entered his divine existence.

BUDDHĀVATĀRA

King *Śuddhodana* of the solar race was ruling the *Śākyas* from the city of *Kapilavāstu*. His queen was *Mahāmāyā*. A son was born to them who was named *Siddhārtha*. Sage *Asita* came to the palace and prophecied that the prince would give up the kingdom and strive for freedom from the sufferings of worldly existence. Eager to see that his son does not renounce the kingdom, the king married him to a beautiful princess *Yaśodharā*, daughter of *Suprabuddha*. The king made deliberate attempts to keep away any unpleasant situation from *Siddhārtha* in order that it may not perturb his mind and kindle spiritual thoughts. He built beautiful palaces for him consisting of rooms suited to different seasons and kept a number of maidens at his service to delight him with music and dance.

Once, *Siddhārtha* was playing with *Devadatta*, his cousin, in the backyard of the palace. *Devadatta* saw a pigeon on the branch of a tree and hit it with a stone. The bird was hurt and fell on the ground. *Siddhārtha* ran towards the bird and caressing it with love and treating the wounds saved its life. *Devadatta* claimed the bird as his as he had caused its fall. *Siddhārtha* disputed his claim and refused to hand it over to him as he had saved its life. In the meanwhile King *Śuddhodana* arrived on the scene. Upon hearing the dispute he ruled that the bird belonged to *Siddhārtha* as he was its saviour. Young *Siddhārtha*, full of compassion, treated the bird until it fully recovered and then set it free.

In course of time, *Yaśodharā* gave birth to a son who was named *Rāhula*. *Siddhārtha* spent many years in the pleasures of royal life with his wife and son. As fate would have it, one day the women of the palace took him to the beautiful groves near the city. The king gave orders to his deputies to keep the afflicted common folk away from the route of the procession. But *Siddhārtha* saw an aged person suffering the afflictions of old age. The charioteer *Candaka* explained to *Siddhārtha* about old age as the natural modification of the body that every one is subject to in time. *Siddhārtha* was moved by the agony of the old man and fears of the cruel hands of time entered his mind. He returned to the palace distressed at the phenomenon of ageing.

The king arranged another excursion to divert *Siddhārtha*'s mind to the pleasant. But this time he saw a person who was terribly sick. *Siddhārtha* was told by *Candaka* about *vyādhis*, diseases, which were part of any living body.

I. Narrate the story depicted in the following illustration.

Buddhāvatāra contd...

Siddhārtha was deeply affected by the sufferings of the sick person and frightened by the calamities that diseases could cause in his life. He could not proceed with the pleasure trip and returned to the palace.

At another time during his travels, he saw a dead body being carried to the crematorium. *Candaka* explained to *Siddhārtha* how death was the culmination of the changes that the human body undergoes and that every living being had to leave the world one day. Upon hearing this, *Siddhārtha* became restless and wanted to find out about the truth of human existence and a solution for human sufferings. He became dispassionate from his royal life and desired to devote himself to the enquiry of truth. He was blessed by a monk who instructed him on the life of a mendicant for gaining liberation.

Siddhārtha was in his twenty-fourth year. One night when everyone was asleep, he had one last look at his wife and son, and mentally taking leave of them, left the palace with *Candaka*. They rode to the banks of River Anoma where *Siddhārtha* removed his jewels and royal robes and gave them to *Candaka*. He instead wore the garb of a mendicant and shaved his head. Requesting *Candaka* to return to the kingdom, he proceeded to walk alone towards *Rājagṛha* in *Magadha*.

Siddhārtha sat in meditation under a bodhi tree in a forest for a number of years. He realised that freedom cannot be gained by fasting or other disciplines, but by enlightening the mind with truth of existence. He pursued his enquiry further until he was totally satisfied with his understanding.

Buddha taught *ahiṃsā*, noninjury, as the basis of righteousness, and *nirvāṇa*, *mokṣa*, as the ultimate end of this life. King *Bimbisāra* became an ardent disciple of Lord *Buddha*. *Buddha's* father and his other family members also visited him and embraced his teachings. Lord *Buddha* taught for forty-five years and finally attained *nirvāṇa* in *Kuśīnagara*.

II. Fill in the blanks with the words below to complete each sentence.

enlightenment	*Śuddhodana*	ascetic
Rāhula	forest	*Yaśodharā*
sheltered	saved	*Śākya*

1. *Siddhārtha* was the son of _______________ the _______________ ruler of *Kapilavāstu.*

2. He led a _______________ life and grew up in luxury.

3. *Siddhārtha*'s wife was _______________ and his son was _______________.

4. King *Śuddhodana* gave the bird to *Siddhārtha* as he had _______________ the bird's life.

5. He saw an old man, a sick man, a corpse and an _______________.

6. *Siddhārtha* left his palace and went to the _______________.

7. He attained _______________ under a Bodhi tree in Bauddha Gaya.

III. Circle the odd one out.

GROUP 1

a) *Siddhārtha*

b) *Gautama*

c) *Buddha*

d) *Rāhula*

GROUP 2

a) *Yaśodharā*

b) *Rāhula*

c) *Gautama*

d) *Kapilavāstu*

GROUP 3

a) sick man

b) corpse

c) ascetic

d) bride

GROUP 4

a) enlightenment

b) Bauddha Gaya

c) meditation

d) mango tree.

KALKYAVATĀRA

Kalkyavatāra is the final *avatāra* which is yet to take place. King *Parīkṣit*, the son of *Abhimanyu*, was the first king at *Hastināpura* after the advent of *Kali-yuga*, an age in the cycle of time when *adharma* prevails. When King *Parīkṣit* ruled the kingdom, he was disturbed by the growing influence of *Kali* in the minds of people. One day he saw a strange incident on the banks of River *Sarasvatī*. There was a dialogue between a bull who was limping on one leg and an emaciated cow who was in tears. They were both lamenting their fate. Suddenly a man arrived on the scene and attacked them with his stick. King *Parīkṣit* intervened and stopped his inhuman behaviour. He listened to the stories of the bull and the cow and discovered that they were none other than Lord *Dharma* and Mother Earth respectively. The man revealed his identity as *Kali* and surrendered to the King. *Parīkṣit* granted one place as an asylum for *Kali*, namely gold. Gold represented money and power devoid of wisdom. From that day onward, *Kali* started living with his companions such as greed, untruth, stealth and hypocrisy in places where wealth existed without wisdom. Such places were gambling, alcoholism, terrorism and so on. Living in these places *Kali* is said to breed *adharma* and destroy the life of a human being.

As *Kali-yuga* advances it is said that unrighteous people would rule the earth and there would be general decline in the universal values. Towards the end of *Kali*, people would lose *śraddhā*, faith, in the scriptures and the Lord and become irreligious. *Artha*, wealth and *kāma*, sense pleasures alone would occupy the minds of people. When *adharma* reaches its heights, the Lord would incarnate as *Kalki*, the son of *Viṣṇuyaśas*, a brahmin in the village of *Śambhala*. He would ride the celestial horse, *Devadatta* and hold a sword in his hand. He would create soldiers and arms at will and destroying the adharmic people would reestablish *dharma* on earth.

Thus a new cycle of time would begin starting with *Satya-yuga*.

I. Find Me

Identify the places on earth where Kali lives and colour them.

II. Help Me

Help Lord Kalki journey through the solar system to reach Mother Earth.

III. Unscramble the words.

1. Y B I M A N U A H

   The father of King *Parīkṣit* was _______________.

2. Ṣ R P K I T I A

   The first ruler of *Kaliyuga* was _______________.

3. *Ṛ Ṣ A K Ṇ*

   King *Parīkṣit* was a devotee of _______________.

4. I K L A

   _______________ lives where the Lord is forgotten.

5. R E H S O

   The *Kalki-avatāra* will come riding on a white _____________.

Avatāra Review

I. Number the *Avatāra* in the correct sequence.

_______ *Kalki*

_______ *Vāmana*

_______ *Rāma*

_______ *Matsya*

_______ *Varāha*

_______ *Kṛṣṇa*

_______ *Kūrma*

_______ *Paraśurāma*

_______ *Narasiṃha*

_______ *Buddha*

II. Match the words.

How did each *avatāra* uphold *dharma*? Match the words in column A and column B.

COLUMN-A		COLUMN-B
1. *Vāmana*	_______	Saved Mother Earth
2. *Rāma*	_______	Destroyed *asura Hiraṇyakaśipu*
3. *Paraśurāma*	_______	Lived a life of *ānanda*
4. *Matsya*	_______	Destroyed King *Bali*'s arrogance
5. *Narasiṃha*	_______	Lived a life of *dharma*
6. *Kūrma*	_______	Will re-establish *dharma* on earth
7. *Varāha*	_______	Offered the nectar of immortality
8. *Kalki*	_______	Lived a life of compassion
9. *Kṛṣṇa*	_______	Destroyed the adharmic *kṣatriyas*
10. *Buddha*	_______	Destroyed the *asura Hayagrīva*

III. Word Search

Look up, down, across and diagonally in the word game and find the *avatāras*. How many *avatāras*, incarnations of Lord *Viṣṇu* are there? ________________

N	A	M	H	S	K	A	L	Z	O	E	K	A
C	N	A	B	I	B	G	V	T	G	O	U	S
E	A	T	O	T	D	*Ā*	D	M	S	Z	P	R
M	*Ṇ*	S	P	A	M	A	T	B	N	A	C	U
I	*Ṣ*	Y	C	A	X	D	I	L	M	P	A	M
Q	*Ṛ*	A	N	A	C	D	A	*Ā*	G	M	P	A
A	K	A	L	K	I	B	R	*Ā*	M	A	A	G
H	M	B	D	U	G	U	O	S	H	R	M	C
Ā	I	L	Z	N	*Ś*	O	R	*M*	A	N	*Ā*	L
R	G	M	I	A	N	A	I	H	D	M	S	O
A	B	K	R	H	N	S	L	M	E	D	A	Q
V	O	A	B	A	A	A	R	B	L	O	L	P
I	P	I	V	R	D	L	K	*Ū*	R	M	A	B
T	A	V	A	B	P	A	H	D	D	U	B	I
A	S	N	V	R	U	M	A	G	L	C	O	Q

Name the three forms of incarnations of Lord *Viṣṇu* which people generally worship at home and in temples.

Made in the USA
Columbia, SC
05 September 2023

22498842R00076